KPD BLUE:
A Decade of Racism, Sexism, and Political Corruption in (and all around) the Kauai Police Department

by
ANTHONY SOMMER

ISBN: 1-4392-0346-6

ISBN-13: 9781439203460

Visit www.booksurge.com to order additional copies.

KPD BLUE

TABLE OF CONTENTS

CHAPTER 1: THE LAP DANCER

"She was on her hands and knees and she was crawling towards me like a cat, licking her lips.

"Then she got up to me. I was seated on a chair and I had my legs spread and she came up between my legs, and she cupped her breasts and she squeezed them together and had my crotch – right around my crotch area.

"Then she pulled her panties to the side, exposed her vagina, and then she started to gyrate on my lap, rubbing her vagina on my crotch area."

That's Officer Alfredo Villanueva of the Honolulu Police Department describing Monica Alves during the trial of Carl Irvin Richie, charged with promoting prostitution and racketeering through his business, Fanta-See Express.

More than a decade later on Kauai, what happened that night, which became known as the "Lap Dancing Incident," casts its long shadow over the Kauai Police Department:

The 10-year political war for the control of the KPD can be traced back to that single incident.

On one side: Two reform police chiefs trying to make the KPD more professional and modern and diverse.

Opposing them: A cabal of entrenched middle managers clinging to the KPD's longtime reputation as a gang of thugs in blue with no respect for the rule of law.

On that night of September 16, 1995, Villanueva and his partner, Officer Jensen Okagawa, were on loan to the KPD from the Honolulu Police Department. Kauai is so small it is very hard for local police to operate undercover without being identified.

The pair of HPD vice officers posed as construction contractors who had just finished a job on Kauai and were having a party at a rented condominium.

Outside was the KPD intelligence squad waiting for a signal from Villanueva to raid the condo and arrest Richie and the women. The two undercover officers wore wires and their conversations with Richie and the women were recorded.

Shortly after 8 p.m., Richie arrived at the condo and handed Villanueva a written contract for three women to perform for one hour in return for $750.

The undercover officers paid Richie $750. He departed and soon returned with stereo equipment and three women: Alves, Riaana Hernandez and Fania Hicks. A fourth woman, Tina Silva, assisted Ritchie.

The two undercover officers testified all three of the women danced, originally topless and later naked, around the room and took turns sitting in the laps of and taking tips from the "customers." Richie collected all the tips from the women.

At one point, Monica Alves, whose role would become much more important later that night, sat naked on Villanueva's lap.

Then Alves did the same for Okagawa, who testified in Richie's trial:

"In this—in this, um, point in her routine, uh, she was completely naked and she sat on my lap with her back facing toward me and, uh, she started grinding her vagina on to the crotch of my pants, simulating sexual intercourse and then, uh, she leaned back on my chest and then grabbed both my hands and placed them on her breasts.

"I removed my hands and then she grabbed them again."

During a break between dance sessions, Villanueva approached Richie.

"I told him that my partner was interested in one of the girls, and I told him – described her, and I said that I think she was introduced as Monique (the name Monica Alves was using that night).

"I told him that – well, he asked what they wanted to do and I asked him if they could disappear for a little while, that he wanted to have sex with her in the bedroom. I turned and looked at my partner and smiled at him.

"Then, he (Richie) turned his back on me and he told me that it's going to cost me an extra $225.

"Officer Okagawa also told him, yeah, that he was interested in Monique and he wanted to have sex with her.

That's when he (Richie) told us it would have to be after the performance and it had to be a private showing."

At the end of the performance, the officers gave the signal and KPD officers entered the condominium and arrested Richie and the four women.

Records seized by KPD showed Richie had conducted 80 similar performances on Kauai.

On Feb. 19, 1996, a jury found Richie guilty of promoting prostitution and racketeering. He was sentenced to five years on the prostitution charge and a concurrent 10 years for racketeering.

On June 25, 1998, the Hawaii Supreme Court ruled Richie could not be convicted of two crimes involving the same act. The racketeering conviction was overturned and his sentence reduced to five years for promoting prostitution.

• • •

CHAPTER 2: KPD'S FINEST

Richie and the four women were taken to the main police station in Lihue, a ramshackle and rambling one-story structure wedged between the ancient state courthouse and Wilcox Elementary School.

Both the police station and the courthouse have since been replaced by modern structures but the people working inside – and, more importantly, the cultures – haven't changed.

Randy Machado was tried in November 1996, on charges of destroying evidence and sexually molesting Alves. He was the only one of the officers charged with a crime to stand trial.

The four women were strip-searched by a woman KPD officer, Darla Abbatiello. Alves later testified that officer Randy Machado said he wanted to conduct the strip search but Abbatiello refused to allow him to do so.

Before the search, Machado went up to Abbatiello, a fashion model before she became a cop, and asked the officer "regarding her breasts and my breasts and whether my breasts were real and whether her breasts were real," Alves testified at Machado's trial.

After she was searched, Alves testified, four of the KPD officers involved in the sting operation took Alves to the watch sergeant's office.

The 1995 arrest of Monica Alves on charges of prostitution and the subsequent sexual abuse of her by Kauai Police Department officers set off a chain of events that rocked the KPD and Kauai County Government for the next decade. Alves is shown here during a recess in her murder trial. She currently is serving a life sentence.

Also present—and the only one wearing a police uniform although the plain clothes undercover officers were carrying guns and badges, was the watch sergeant—Sgt. Mel Rapozo.

Alves testified Rapozo did not participate in what happened next, but he was in the office the entire time, smiling and laughing and making comments and doing nothing to stop the other officers.

Alves said Randy Machado closed the office door, which led outside to a parking lot.

The officers first put a KPD uniform hat on Alves' head, she testified. At this point, she was still handcuffed.

"Randy Machado said he wanted to see my breasts. He unbuttoned it (her dress)," Alves said.

"I was scared to object to anything from that point on. I asked:'Are you guys trying to set me up?'" Alves testified.

She said one of the officers took a Polaroid camera and some film out of a locker in the office and began taking pictures.

Alves testified at this time she was still wearing a bra and g-string panties.

"Randy Machado grabbed my breasts and my private area. I told him to stop.

"He said he thought my breasts were beautiful and they were real and told the others to come and check them out," she told the court.

At that point, she testified, Machado picked Alves up. He sat in a chair and placed Alves on his lap and spread her legs with his legs, fondling her breasts and vaginal area while pictures were taken.

"I went along without screaming or crying out because I was scared," Alves testified.

"They can do anything they want, anywhere they want because they're cops," she testified. "In other words, they could kill me there if they wanted to and they actually thought they could get away with it and that they'd done this before."

"They could maybe say I tried to hurt them and have me hurt. He (Machado) made it very clear to me that – you know what? – He could have people hurt and it's just as simple as that in his position. That he could have people hurt," Alves told the court.

Alves said Machado then picked her up again and bent her over the arm of an office chair, pulled her panties to the side and explored her vaginal area.

"He said he thought it was beautiful and invited the others to take a look," she said.

Then Machado looked closely at her vagina. "He said I still had miles to go."

Alves testified Machado picked her up again, placed her on the watch sergeant's desk and removed her handcuffs.

Rapozo, the watch sergeant, watched and did nothing to stop Machado.

"He asked me to do my crawl. He said he had seen it in my show," Alves said.

She said she couldn't crawl on the desk but "posed in a crawling position" while the officers took more pictures.

The KPD officers then allowed Alves to dress. When she was clothed, she testified, Machado grabbed her again from behind.

"He started grinding his penis on my buttocks. I felt it," Alves said. Both she and Machado were wearing clothes at that time.

"He said he didn't know how he was going to explain to his wife how he came all over himself," Alves testified.

The KPD released Alves "pending investigation" shortly before dawn.

KPD Sgt. Clinton Bettencourt, who testified Alves sometimes served as an informant for him, gave Alves a ride home to her husband and two children.

The sergeant testified that she told him very briefly about what happened and gave a description of Randy Machado but he didn't ask Alves any questions.

"She was crying. I didn't want to push it," Bettencourt explained to the court.

The sergeant testified he did not ask any questions of other police officers when he returned to the police station and did not report what Alves told him.

Willie Ihu told a similar tale from the witness stand. He saw no evil, but he didn't look very hard.

Ihu was a sergeant in 1995 and was the second in command of the sting operation that nabbed Monica Alves.

In the trial of Randall Machado, Ihu testified that Machado came to Ihu's office about 1:30 a.m. and told him, "Willie, you better go look in the back. Some of the girls are running around. Some of them may be naked. Some of the guys are taking their pictures." He also told Ihu the officers were fondling the women.

Machado did not tell Ihu he was the main culprit. What he was attempting to do, of course, was lay down a smoke screen to cover up what he had done.

Ihu said he went back where the women were being held in a lunch room, saw that all of them were dressed and then went back to his office.

Ihu admitted he didn't ask any of the women or any of the officers any questions.

Ihu didn't get involved and wasn't disciplined.

Machado's defense attorney, Bill Feldhacker, presented a very different story.

Feldhacker introduced a statement from one of the dancers, Fania Hicks, who said she saw Alves go into the watch sergeant's office with the officers and she saw Alves removing her own clothes and crawl on the table.

Hicks said it was Alves who closed the door to the office, not any of the officers.

Kelly Lau, a cousin of Alves's, testified Alves had been with her the afternoon before the sting operation. She said Alves at that time was drunk and under the influence of crystal meth.

At 4 a.m., after Alves had been released, Lau said she received a telephone call from Alves, who said she was home alone and she wanted Lau to come over to her house and party. Lau said she brought four people with her, but none of them testified to substantiate her story.

Lau said that, at Alves' house, Alves was topless and wearing a G-string and taking drugs. Lau testified Alves told her that she had voluntarily not only put on a police hat but also a police shirt, gun belt and baton and posed for pictures.

"She was bragging about it," Alau said. "She thought it was a joke."

In his closing argument, Feldhacker conceded his client Machado had told police internal investigators: "I know it was wrong. I know it was unethical."

But he said Machado repeatedly denied Alves had been forced to do anything.

And Feldhacker argued Alves wasn't acting out of fear.

"She wasn't afraid of police officers," Feldhacker told the court. "She's learned long ago how to manipulate them in a sexual way."

Fifth Circuit Court Judge George Masuoka found Randy Machado guilty of destroying evidence: the nude photos of Monica Alves taken in Rapozo's Office, which he had run through a shredder in the KPD Records Section.

But the judge tossed out the charges against all the officers that they had molested Alves.

Masuoka called the officers' actions "wrong, immoral, unethical and, last, but not least, stupid," but he ruled prosecutors were unable to prove that the officers took sexual liberties with Alves against her will.

Masuoka said Alves' testimony was inconsistent with statements she had previously made. Lau's testimony was suspect, Masuoka said. But the question of reasonable doubt remained and that was enough for acquittal on the sexual assault charge.

"Under the circumstances, the state has not met the burden of proving Ms. Alves did not consent. The state has not proven coercion," the judge said.

The three charges of sexual abuse against Machado fell into a loophole in Hawaii law.

If a state corrections officer had sexually touched an inmate, with or without consent, the crime would be a felony.

But the law did not extend to county police officers and arrested suspects who consent to or who are forced to have sex with the cops who operate the temporary holding cells at the police stations.

The statute since has been amended to include prisoners being held by police officers. But it was not on the books at the time of Alves's arrest, the judge noted.

"It should not be permitted and it should be a felony, whether with or without consent," Masuoka said. "This conduct should not be accepted or tolerated in our community."

And in a not-at-all subtle hint to Police Chief George Freitas to take stern disciplinary action, Masuoka added: "I believe the chief should get the message."

Chief Freitas did and fired the officers.

But the SHOPO, the State of Hawaii Organization of Police Officers, the police union, stood in his way.

· · ·

CHAPTER 3: AFTERSHOCKS

Revelations of continuing racism, sexism and dishonesty continue to haunt the KPD. They all circle back to the arrest of Monica Alves.

Immediately following the Lap Dancing Incident, newly appointed Police Chief George Freitas fired patrolmen Randy Machado, Todd Tanaka and Sgt. Mel Rapozo. The two other officers accused of molesting Alves resigned.

Machado, Tanaka and Rapozo filed union complaints. The case was submitted to binding arbitration and KPD was forced to reinstate all three.

One of the arbitrators who ordered the officers reinstated was Kauai lawyer Max Graham, an attorney for many of the biggest developers on Kauai.

Rather than take an ethical "zero tolerance" stand, Graham chose to bow down to SHOPO and the local politicians who wanted the officers reinstated.

Because of the nature of his wealthy mainland clients and their need for many Kauai County permits, it was in Graham's best interests to please and placate the county government on Kauai.

So, Graham placed the blame not on the officers who were directly involved but on their superiors who never were named or disciplined.

"It further appears," Graham wrote in his findings, "that more senior officers knew or should have known that better control was warranted."

The logic seems to be that KPD officers and sergeants couldn't possibly have been expected to know that stripping, fondling and photographing a woman they had just arrested was wrong unless a senior department official was standing right there to tell them so.

Rapozo turned down reinstatement, which would have required him to accept a demotion to patrolman, and instead became a private investigator. He later was elected to the Kauai County Council where he has become the KPD's loudest and most passionate critic.

Despite Judge Masuoka's feigned outrage, he sentenced Machado to only 30 days in jail for destroying evidence. Machado could have received a two-year term.

Shortly after he returned to duty, Machado was named "Officer of the Month" by the Kauai Police Commission.

In 1999 he was awarded the "Top Cop Award" by the Hawaii Joint Police Association.

Clearly, there was no shame in the police community about the Alves incident.

Machado later died in a freak skate-boarding accident in front of his home. He received a full-blown police funeral and was accorded a hero's obituary in the local newspaper. There was no mention of the lap dancer.

The news media in Hawaii develops a highly selective sense of recall when a controversial public figure dies. The evil they have done conveniently disappears when the obituaries are written.

Even though the trial of Randy Machado was recorded on video tape that is public record, it never has been presented to the people of Kauai before this book was printed.

There would be a striking similarity to the reportage of Macahdo's death when Kauai Mayor Bryan Baptiste died in office a decade later.

Baptiste's many controversial and ethically questionable deeds and decisions (he was re-elected to a second term by only two votes) vanished as far as the reporters writing his obituaries were concerned. In death, he was universally hailed as "The Aloha Mayor."

Proper observance of local custom, perhaps, but astonishingly poor journalism, which is supposed to be about presenting the facts to the public.

Gone from public view but certainly not forgotten, The "Lap Dancing Incident" carried a curse, tainting everyone involved in it. Its evil spell continues today.

Alves sued the KPD and the county for sexual harassment and received a $250,000 settlement, a measure of how desperately Kauai County wanted (and still always wants) to avoid a potentially humiliating public civil trial.

Most of the money Alves was paid by Kauai County went up her nose and into her arms in the form of drug purchases.

The settlement contained a confidentiality agreement that was insisted on by Kauai County and that was totally illegal. Settlements paid by tax dollars are supposed to be public record.

But, there is much in Kauai County that is supposed to be public that Kauai County government keeps secret.

And no one, certainly not the Hawaii news media, challenges Kauai County in court.

Shortly afterward, Alves and her husband Mitch Peralto were convicted of the brutal torture and murder of Alves' niece, a KPD drug informant.

Four adults at the house where the victim was being held witnessed the couple beat, bind and gag Kimberly Washington Cohen, 23, and drive off with her in their car on July 11, 1997. The witnesses did nothing.

It was only later, when the owner returned home, that the police were called.

Apparently, Alves knew Washington Cohen was a confidential informant (although KPD records showed she never provided them any useful information) and believed she had tipped off the police. KPD vice officers had stopped Alves and searched her for drugs.

While beating Washington Cohen, Alves tried to seal her lips shut with fingernail glue, telling her, according to a witness, "You're never going to be able to talk again."

The four witnesses watched Alves and Peralto bind Washington Cohen's arms, ankles and beasts, gag her mouth so tightly "her face was deformed," duct-tape a blanket over her head and torso and drag her struggling into the back seat of their car and drive away.

The next day, police found the woman's body in a shallow grave less than a mile from the house where she had been beaten. The cause of death was suffocation.

Alves, sobbing when she heard the guilty verdict, and Peralto were convicted and sentenced to life in prison with no possibility of parole.

If Monica Alves, from her prison cell, is aware of all the twisted turns KPD has taken ever since her arrest for lap dancing, she must be laughing at all of them.

· · ·

CHAPTER 4: KAUAI STYLE

In 1998, Mary Thronas, chairwoman of the Kauai County Council, veteran politician and member of a well-known cattle ranching family, had just filed her papers to run for mayor of Kauai against incumbent Mayor Maryanne Kusaka.

After handing her nominating petitions to the county clerk, Thronas ambled over to the local newspaper for the obligatory interview.

She sat down in an office with the managing editor and a reporter who asked her how much she expected to spend on her campaign.

"Last time, each candidate spent about $50,000," she said. "I'm going to try to Jew that down to about $30,000."

The reporter just kept nodding his head and scribbled it down. He was well aware that Jew is a noun, not a verb or adjective.

Thronas, who was part-Hawaiian, had strong support from the Native Hawaiian community, which likes to label itself "The Host Culture."

In fact, Native Hawaiians (*Kanaka* is the term they prefer) have become, thanks to America's peculiar brand of expansionism (the word colonialism never was used, although in Hawaii's case it certainly applied) a century ago, a conquered people and a small minority in its own land.

The swing vote on Kauai really belongs to the Filipino community, the poorest but most numerous ethnic group. In recent elections, it is the Filipino vote that has inevitably proven to be the deciding factor and the Filipinos are courted openly by Kauai's politicians.

Kusaka was popular among Filipinos. Thronas conceded that would be a tough hill to climb.

"Well, the mayor has been handing out part-time jobs to the Filipino community for a long time. That way, she can hire lots of them for a few hours a week without having to bother with civil service and the unions."

No fool, the incumbent mayor.

But then Thronas added:

"You go over to the county building and it's so packed with Filipinos, it looks like a Manila taxicab."

Goodbye Filipino vote. Goodbye mayor's office.

Hello, big story.

The Associated Press picked it up and Thronas's racist comments were reprinted all over Hawaii.

The National Public Radio station in Honolulu (which has transmitters on every island except Kauai, ironically) used it as a topic for a statewide call-in show.

The transplanted mainland limousine liberals and third-generation hippies on Maui, of course, phoned to vent their politically correct furor at Thronas. The B'nai B'rith Anti-Defamation League (ADL) sent Thronas a sharp rebuke the same day the story appeared. Who would have guessed a board member of the ADL, a retired doctor, lived on Kauai?

But those were all *haoles*, outsiders, mainlanders and they are a minority in Hawaii, comprising about 40 percent of Kauai's population.

The majority is local and an astounding number defended what Thronas said.

"That's just the way we talk," was said over and over. "It doesn't mean we discriminate against people."

Thronas's response fell a bit short of an apology: "How did I know the reporter was Jewish?"

The use of racist terms by local KPD officers is not unusual. Almost every KPD officer was born and raised on Kauai where racist slurs are part of every day vocabulary among locals..

During Randy Machado's trial, Monica Alves testified that after she had been released the next morning, she made several calls asking when Richie would be released and how much bail he would be required to pay.

Machado answered one of the calls.

"'Why would you want to help that nigger (Richie is African-American) out?'" Alves testified that Machado asked her.

A month later, after she had been indicted, Alves was arrested again and booked into jail by Machado.

At Machado's trial, she testified: "He told me I had two choices: I could go to jail for five years and not see my kids or I could help him 'get the nigger.'"

There is no county or KPD written policy about the use of racial epithets. No Kauai government employee ever has been disciplined for using them.

And it's made worse by the absence of the normal checks and balances found in government in the most of United States.

The civil rights revolution on the mainland was led by the courts. Brown vs. the Board of Education, the 1954 U.S. Supreme Court decision that ended racial segregation in the schools, was the foundation on which the outlawing of racism was built.

Ten years later came the Civil Rights Act.

If anyone on Kauai noticed, it still is hard to tell.

There has been no similar trend toward diversity in either the Kauai court or Kauai County government.

To a great extent, the rogue nature of the executive (mayor) and legislature (County Council) on Kauai were validated and endorsed by the judicial branch.

Up until very recently, the law on the Garden Island, as Kauai is known, was determined by a single judge, who was a local politician first and a jurist second.

The judge's comments from the bench often were seasoned with racist statements. A defense attorney's characterization of his Portuguese client as an honest citizen during sentencing typically brought a comment from the bench: "You're wrong, counsel, I know that Portagee!"

The term "Law West of Honolulu" often is used by Oahu lawyers to describe Kauai's court, a reference to the sign that hung over the door of Judge Roy Bean's saloon/courthouse in Vinagaroon, Texas: "Law West of the Pecos."

It's not a term intended to be flattering to Kauai.

Kauai had its own Judge Bean. His name was Fifth Circuit Judge George Masuoka. He was Japanese-American (AJA or American of Japanese Ancestry is the term they prefer), an ethic group that considers itself elite and, in fact, the ruling class in Hawaii.

Masuoka, who retired in December 2006, was the scourge of criminals and the devoted friend of the Kauai County government (and an even closer personal friend of the chief justice of the Hawaii Supreme Court, which is how he kept his job).

He almost never gave probation. According to statistics published annually by the state, Masuoka handed out criminal sentences that, by a huge margin, were harsher than any judge in the state.

Whether intentional or not, Masuoka's "law and order" stance in criminal cases was giving a green light to the KPD to violate the Constitutional rights of citizens however and whenever they chose.

In civil cases, Masuoka almost always sided with Kauai County when citizens brought suit against it. That was another signal to KPD that just about anything its officers did would be considered legal.

As a result of Masuoka's foot dragging (and, to be fair, his heavy case load; he has been replaced by two judges) lawsuits against Kauai County tended to stall for many years.

The county's strategy was to hope the plaintiffs would give up in frustration or from lack of money to pay lawyers, or they would simply die of old age waiting for a trial date.

The county has plenty of money to pay lawyers and lots of patience.

The playing field isn't at all level in the courthouse on Kauai.

That's why, whenever they could, plaintiffs' attorneys steered their cases against Kauai County toward federal court in Honolulu.

If the cases were filed in U.S. District Court, Kauai County almost always offered a huge settlement rather than going to trial. Kauai County knew it would lose in federal court and they certainly didn't want public trials with witnesses testifying about the facts of the cases.

When a court like Kauai's Fifth Circuit has a monopoly on justice the only judge abdicates his role as a sentinel guarding the "Rule of Law," the politicians, the bureaucrats and, most important, the police happily follow.

Because the presiding judge for so many years refused to condemn or punish local officials who bent or broke the law, the government of Kauai County operated outside the law and was damn proud of it.

Kauai is a cultural (and judicial) (and political) backwater but it's one of the most famous and popular tourist destinations in the world.

There are only 58,000 permanent residents on Kauai but more than one million tourists – many of them owners of time shares and second homes on the island and who pay taxes on Kauai – visit every year.

Ask visitors their thoughts about racism on Kauai and the tourists say it doesn't exist.

In the words of one part-time Kauai resident from Missouri:

"The bag boys at the golf course are great guys. And I give them big tips."

. . .

CHAPTER 5: MARYANNE KUSAKA

Mayor Maryanne Kusaka never lacked for style.

Kusaka's clothes always were carefully tailored, formal and decidedly pastel. Her hair never revealed a single stray strand. She invariably wore a brightly colored scarf on her neck to disguise the loose skin waddle of age on her throat.

Her manners, in public at least, were very courtly. She had a warm smile. She only rarely displayed anger in public. Her rants tended toward scolding rather than verbal assaults.

It was in substance and ethical stature that Kusaka was lacking. The first thing she did after raising her hand and taking the oath of office as mayor was to start selling jewelry out of the mayor's office.

A retired public school teacher who never held an elected office before becoming mayor, Kusaka learned how to run Kauai County during her years as administrative assistant to Mayor Anthony "Uncle Tony" Kunimura.

On Kauai, the administrative assistant is not, as the title would imply on the mainland, a secretary. Kusaka was the unelected deputy mayor and first in line as heir to the throne if Mayor Kunimura was incapacitated.

Kunimura, who ruled Kauai in the early and mid 1980s, easily was the most flamboyant mayor in the island's history. He didn't bother very much with obeying the law because, well, who would challenge him?

When Kusaka became mayor in 1994, she commissioned (but didn't pay for; the taxpayers did that) a bust of Kunimura, who had died by then, and his bronze image holds the place of honor in the center of the courtyard of the county office complex.

"Uncle Tony" ran Kauai in the old style: Reward your friends and punish your enemies.

"Auntie Maryanne," his protégé, was an apt pupil. She took care of her supporters and loosed the hounds, the county bureaucrats (including the cops), on her detractors.

Kusaka was a lifelong Democrat until she ran for mayor.

In the 1994 Democratic primary, Jimmy Tehada, a veteran County Council member, defeated the incumbent mayor, JoAnn Yukimura.

It wasn't that the voters loved Tehada. They were angry at Yukimura.

Kauai's recovery from 1992's Hurricane Iniki was slow, largely because of the incompetence of the entrenched county bureaucracy, which Yukimura had inherited.

Yukimura brought in many talented department heads but they could not break through the inertia caused by strong unions and civil service protection. And many of her cabinet members were *haoles*, mainlanders, and no matter how competent, they were resented by locals, particularly locals who worked for the county.

So, Yukimura took the heat at election time. She took the loss very personally and left Kauai for several years. Later she returned and won election to the County Council.

That meant Tehada, who had knocked her off, was not a particularly popular candidate in the general election. He had been a convenient alternative to Yukimura in the primary. But Tehada was very vulnerable to a well-financed challenger in the general election..

Backed by Kauai businessmen and running as the heir to Tony Kunimura, Kusaka re-registered as a Republican and won the general election.

To run the county and take charge of the recovery from Hurricane Iniki, Kusaka brought in retired Navy Capt. Bob Mullins, the former commander of the Pacific Missile Range Facility on Kauai as her administrative assistant.

The US Navy in general and Bob Mullins in particular had become folk heroes in the aftermath of Iniki. The missile range provided help first and asked for permission later. After the recovery, Mullins brought stacks of documents to the mayor's office to be signed. He wanted cover to show they had "requested" the aid he and the Navy provided.

Kusaka covered Mullins and, when he retired and she was elected, she gave him a job.

Mullins had his own political base—the almost exclusively white and exclusively Republican Navy League, a booster club for the Navy—and that helped Kusaka gain entry into her new political party.

Later, she replaced Mullins (who found himself cozy employment with a defense contractor, as do many military officers involved in the testing and evaluation trade).

Kusaka brought in a local CPA, Wally Rezentes, who shortly afterward filed for bankruptcy because of the failure of his own business.

Rezentes's son, Wally Jr., was hired as the county's director of finance. Nepotism, the hiring of relatives, is totally accepted practice in Kauai County government.

Led by both Wally Sr. and Wally Jr., Kusaka's top aides worked to recover the island from the remaining ravages of Hurricane Iniki and, most importantly, to fend off the Federal Emergency Management Agency (FEMA).

Kauai County was somewhat extravagant in billing FEMA for repairing hurricane damage, including upgrading some county facilities from pre-hurricane condition. Wood buildings were replaced with concrete structures. FEMA was not amused.

Meanwhile, Mayor Kusaka went on the road to boost tourism.

Kusaka loved to travel, and she freely spent huge sums of county money to take dancers and singers to travel-agent trade shows all over the world. A genuinely accomplished and talented singer and hula dancer herself, Kusaka performed whenever and wherever she could find a stage.

After 1992's Hurricane Iniki, the mayor's travels to promote Kauai arguably helped the recovery of the tourism industry. Already popular with locals, Kusaka's efforts to attract visitors cemented her image as the poster child of the tourism industry.

In typical Kauai style, locals (including the local newspaper) never questioned how much of their money she was spending on her junkets.

Why weren't the resort hotels and airlines and tour companies she was promoting picking up her tab? No one on Kauai, especially the press, was even mildly curious.

In 1998, Kusaka declared the tourism industry fully recovered. Also, in 1998, the county spent $5,603 to send Kusaka (the figure doesn't include her entourage) on marketing trips.

If the tourist industry was fixed, it would be logical to assume the mayor's sales trips could be reduced in the coming years.

Yet in 1999, Kusaka's travel budget almost tripled to $13,082. She ranked second (behind Honolulu's Mayor Jeremy Harris) among Hawaii mayors for travel spending that year. The mayors of Maui County and Hawaii County weren't even close.

By far her most extravagant trip in 1999 was to the American Society of Travel Agents trade show in Paris. She was Hawaii's sole representative.

Kauai County has a strict policy that employees traveling at taxpayer expense must fly tourist class. But Kusaka flew first class all the way (her economic planning director Gini Kapali sat back in tourist).

Kusaka, in fact, liked everything first class.

Despite the fact that—after Mullins' departure—Kusaka's cabinet lacked any white faces, the mayor had an affinity for wealthy *haole* investors who were willing to court (and, if widely-believed rumor is correct, gladly pay for) her favor.

Kealia Kai is a subdivision of multi-million-dollar homes built on huge lots along a bluff overlooking the ocean on the windward side of Kauai. It also is a gated community, which is very rare on Kauai. The gates are considered a slap in the face of local people.

The land previously had been part of a sugar plantation. The lots were listed on the tax rolls as agricultural property, meaning the property taxes on the land would be virtually zero for the new gentleman farms.

Justin and Michele Hughes, a California couple who had developed similar projects in Colorado, represented themselves as the developers of Kealia Kai on Kauai's east shore just north of Kapaa.

It later turned out another part-time Kauai resident and full-time developer, Thomas McCloskey, was the real developer of the property; a fact the Hughes couple purposely avoided mentioning in public filings.

When a reporter stumbled over McCloskey's name on a document at a state office and called Michele Hughes asking what that was all about, she blurted out: "His name wasn't supposed to be on anything!"

Michele Hughes and Maryanne Kusaka became best friends.

While a pile of applications involving Kealia Kai still were pending action before the Kauai Planning Commission, Kusaka called a press conference to introduce Michele Hughes and sing the praises of Kealia Kai.

When a reporter pointed out that it might be unethical for a mayor to be shilling for a development awaiting action by a county regulatory board, Kusaka responded by giving the reporter a dirty look, called "the stink eye" in Hawaii Pidgin.

Kusaka had her own weekly television show on cable television (paid for by the taxpayers) and her sole guest the following week was Michele Hughes.

They were so tight that during one Planning Commission meeting, Wally Rezentes Sr., Kusaka's top aide, actually was carrying Michele Hughes's purse.

The Kauai County Council, Kauai County Planning Commission and the Kauai County Police Commission meetings are televised and the mayor and the mayor's staff watch them live on closed-circuit television.

Even if the mayor is not in the meeting room, the threat of retaliation is only as far away as the nearest television camera, and the Council members and commission members know it.

Kusaka also provided a fine example of how a Kauai mayor can enlist her police department to benefit her friends.

The beach below Kealia Kai is called Donkey Beach and it had for decades been a gay nude beach. Although nude sunbathing was illegal, that prohibition previously had a very low ranking in the law enforcement scheme of things on Kauai.

Suddenly, Kusaka had the KPD running off the gay nudists on a regular basis to please the developers of Kealia Kai. Mr. and Mrs. Hughes (and, as it later was revealed, Tom McCloskey) didn't think the sight of naked men was helping their chances of selling a "million-dollar view."

Similarly, there was a straight nude beach—called Secret Beach, although there are directions to it in every tourist guidebook—right below and in full view of the Hughes's hillside home in Kilauea.

Suddenly, under orders from the mayor, the KPD was rounding up nude sunbathers there as well.

It was the issue of beach patrols that caused the first major rift between Kusaka and KPD Chief George Freitas.

The Hugheses offered to donate all-terrain vehicles to the KPD, but only if Freitas provided KPD officers to drive them and only if the ATVs were used exclusively to patrol Donkey Beach below Kealia Kai to arrest gay nudists.

Freitas said he would gladly take the donated ATVs, but only if he decided when and where on the island they would be used. He was not willing to provide tax-funded private security patrols for the Hugheses.

Kusaka was embarrassed and she was angry. It is highly likely that it was at this point she began to plot and scheme to get herself a police chief who would do what she told him to do.

Mayor Maryanne Kusaka headed a full-on witch hunt to get KPD Chief Freitas, trying to convince the Kauai Police Commission to fire Freitas for hindering the prosecution of a KPD officer accused of sexually molesting his step-daughter. In the end, the officer was acquitted, Freitas was found guilty of giving his girlfriend a ride in his police car and yelling at one of his assistant chiefs. He kept his job.

Only after all the state and county permits were issued did McCloskey jump out of the woodpile and announce himself as the actual developer of Kealia Kai. Justin and Michele Hughes were just fronting for him and Michele certainly had done her job winning the mayor's friendship.

The mayor, quite naturally, immediately began snuggling up to McCloskey as well.

For a long time, rumors abounded that Kusaka had been paid off with a lot at Kealia Kai. There never was anything in the state or county records to indicate that there was any truth to the oft-repeated allegation. But the rumored payoff was and still is widely believed.

Kusaka also was close friend of Jimmy Pflueger, a retired and very wealthy Honolulu Honda dealer turned land developer on Kauai's north shore. His family had owned land there for more than a century.

Pflueger, often driving the heavy construction equipment himself, was clearing the land and building roads for yet another subdivision for the rich and famous on a bluff overlooking the ocean. In the background are rugged mountains often seen in movies shot on Pflueger's property.

Pflueger had an "arrangement" with Kusaka that was quite unique. The mayor's office served as a sort of alarm system for Pflueger.

If anyone called any Kauai County department to complain about Pflueger's activities and question whether he had permits and was following the law, they got an instant response.

The return call came not from the Planning Department, not from the county engineer, not from the mayor, but from Pflueger himself. Usually within an hour of the original complaint, Pflueger was on the phone with the irate citizen.

Pflueger had made a deal with Kusaka that if any citizen called to complain about any of his pet projects, the complaint would be passed on directly to him by her top aide, Wally Rezentes. Pflueger reckoned, usually correctly, that he could calm them down with his used-car-salesman charm.

The county officials never would investigate the complaints against Pflueger. Kusaka had granted him an informal immunity from county regulation.

That was just fine until Pflueger's excavation to build a road from the lots where he planned to build luxury homes to Pilaa Beach collapsed in a mudslide during a heavy rain storm. The mud buried a coral reef.

Pflueger ended up paying the largest penalty ever imposed by the U.S. Environmental Protection Agency against an individual: $7.5 million.

He also paid the largest state pollution fine in Hawaii's history: $4 million.

The Pilaa mudslide was only the beginning.

More recently, on May 14, 2006, a dam on Pflueger's property burst in another rain storm, creating an 18-foot wall of water that hurtled downstream, wiping out 100 feet of the only highway serving the area, knocking two buildings completely off their foundations and killing seven people downstream.

Authorities still are investigating to determine whether Pflueger had covered over the dam's spillway with dirt, when the spillway was intended as a safety valve to keep the dam from overfilling.

Kauai County, which at Kusaka's urging gave Pflueger free rein and never inspected his many projects, played a role in both of those disasters by failing to enforce the law.

Kusaka's firm belief that the rules do not apply to her finally went a bit too far in 2001.

Annoyed that the County Council refused to grant her a pay raise, Kusaka used her authority to transfer funds within her own office to give herself a new car.

Kusaka for years had been driving her personal Cadillac on county business and received a $4,000 annual travel allowance.

In 2001, without telling the County Council, she quadrupled her own travel allowance and paid $16,000 in county funds to lease a bright red Chrysler luxury car for the balance of her term. The car was strictly for Kusaka's use and the lease specified it would be returned at the end of her term and not made available to the next mayor.

The car was leased, without any bidding, from the automobile dealer who had been her campaign chairman in the previous election. "Sole source" purchases are not uncommon in Kauai County, often in violation of state procurement laws and regulations requiring bids on government purchases.

The Kauai County Council, hardly a tower of ethics and virtue itself, learned of the mayor's new car at a budget briefing.

The Council members had a few years before given the county departments authority to transfer funds with their own agencies without Council approval. In return, each agency, including the mayor's office, was supposed to provide an annual self-evaluation and set goals for the coming year.

Under Kusaka, the money freely was shuffled within the county offices but the goals never were set and the evaluations never completed.

Council members were so angry that Kusaka misused the new budget powers they granted her that they stripped the mayor of all the discretionary spending power.

Ultimately, she turned in the Chrysler and went back to driving her Caddy.

Despite her socializing with wealthy *haole* developers, Kusaka remained popular with locals. This was partly because she provided them with jobs, but also because she "talked stink" about white people when she believed no one would hear her.

"I used to go to cabinet meetings and I was dumbfounded by the racist statements the mayor would repeatedly make at almost every meeting," said former Police Chief George Freitas.

The police chief is not appointed by the mayor but by the Police Commission. The police chief was considered a *de facto* cabinet member and expected to attend department head meetings, largely to be handy when Kusaka wanted to chew him out at cabinet meetings.

Even one of Kusaka's closest aides, who is white, said the same of her boss.

"When she would go into one of her rants about *haoles*, I had to wonder what color she thought I was," said Beth Tokioka, who served as Kusaka's press secretary and later become Mayor Bryan Baptiste's economic planning director.

Tokioka is Caucasian and grew up in Flint, Michigan. She was married to a Japanese-American politician Jimmy Tokioka, now a member of the state legislature, whom Kusaka treats as a son. Though now divorced, her ticket into local society and in county politics now is permanently punched.

Tokioka proved doggedly loyal to both Kusaka and later to Mayor Bryan Baptiste. And it showed. Honesty in her relations with the press was not among her virtues.

"I like Beth but she has some serious ethical blind spots," said Dennis Wilken, a former reporter for The Garden Island, Kauai's local newspaper.

Bill Dahle, the senior reporter on the island, now retired, once told Tokioka to her face that no reporter on Kauai ever believed a word she said because she was so devoted to Kusaka.

Kusaka often called Beth Tokioka "my soul mate."

Other *haoles* in the Kusaka Administration, however, were decidedly unwelcome.

A case in point was in 2002 when Kusaka forced Kauai Film Commissioner Judy Drosd to quit after 10 years on the job, during which she played a major role in the filming of all three *Jurassic Park* movies on the island.

Drosd, a *haole*, had been hired by the previous mayor, JoAnn Yukimura, a liberal Stanford attorney who brought in quite a few talented administrators from the mainland. Most of the outsiders left when Yukimura was defeated for re-election, but not Drosd.

Drosd was a 20-year veteran of the television and motion picture business and previously had been the vice president in charge of production for HBO.

In terms of Big League talent and savvy and charm, Drosd was by far the class act in Kauai County government.

Judy Drosd, a former top executive with HBO and Kauai's film commissioner for a decade was forced out by Mayor Maryanne Kusaka and replaced by a commissioner with no background in the film industry.

With millions of dollars for the island's economy at risk, balancing the needs of demanding film producers, greedy landowners who want huge sums to provide film locations, and egotistic movie stars seeking special treatment is no easy act.

When Drosd left Kauai in 2002, she was immediately hired by newly-elected Gov. Linda Lingle to head the state Arts, Film and Entertainment Division. She kept her home on Kauai and commuted to Honolulu every day.

Drosd's departure resulted directly from the Kusaka's very shabby treatment of her. Her departure was a tragedy for the island and film-making on Kauai never really has recovered.

Parroting the mayor, Press Secretary Tokioka took it upon herself to play down the loss of Drosd.

Tokioka said in an interview: The film commissioner was "nothing more than a glorified tour guide."

She added Drosd "hung around for 10 years only so she would be vested in the county's retirement system." From all indications, Drosd, who owned a great deal of property on Kauai, was not in need of a government pension.

Kusaka replaced Drosd with Tiffani Lizama, the marketing director for the Kauai Food Bank who had no experience in the film industry.

Worse, Lizama chose as her show business guru the builder of a recording studio in Kapaa that turned out to be nothing more than a means for scamming investors. He fled the island leaving a large number of angry investors in his wake.

The important point to Kusaka was that Lizama, though a *haole*, was married to a local Kauai Fire Department captain who was one of the mayor's pets. Again, marriage to a local is a *haole's* ticket into the club.

Kusaka's dislike of whites and especially whites who opposed her in public was put on full public display in 2002.

There is a gaggle of activists who show up at every Kauai County Council meeting to complain, usually quite correctly, how inept and unethical most county agencies are.

They call themselves the "nit-pickers," a tag intended to be derogatory that was pinned on them by the editor of the local paper. They wear it as a badge of honor.

All are *haoles*. Locals would never speak out against the government.

County Council meetings were given live gavel-to-gavel coverage (except, of course, for the many executive sessions) on Hoike, the public access cable television network.

In addition to the Council meetings, Kauai County paid Hoike $40,000 a year to provide a video crew and transmit the mayor's weekly television show, which was nothing but a propaganda opportunity and was scripted by Beth Tokioka.

(Kusaka also did a weekly radio "interview" with a Kauai "newsman" on a local radio station. Both the questions and Kusaka's answers were written by Beth Tokioka.)

The line between Kusaka and the activist community was drawn during her first term.

A decades-old dispute between north shore residents reached the boiling point in 1997 and 1998.

Tour boat companies were hauling thousands of visitors every day on sight-seeing trips along the spectacular Na Pali Coast.

The tour boats ran out of Hanalei on Kauai's north shore, technically a harbor but not nearly large enough to accommodate the huge number of tour boats and tourist vehicles running in and out of what is, arguably, the most beautiful bay in the world.

Kusaka lined up with the boat operators, part of her beloved tourism industry.

That put her on the opposite side from the environmental activists, an unlikely coalition of white North Shore environmentalists and pro-sovereignty Native Hawaiians who claimed the boats were destroying the bay, the river and the town. They wanted the tour boats out of Hanalei Bay.

The issue was so contentious that one joint state and county public hearing droned on for 18 hours of passionate speech-making from representatives of both sides, televised on Hoike, of course..

It finally was decided in 1998 by Gov. Ben Cayetano, whose speech-writer was—not coincidentally—a *haole* environmentalist from Kauai.

Cayetano was, at the time, in a desperate fight for a second term against former Maui Mayor Linda Lingle.

Cayetano was a Democrat and needed the liberal north shore Kauai vote. Lingle and Kusaka were Republicans.

Cayetano simply pulled the plug on the tour boats and Kusaka.

He ordered them out of Hanalei and forced them to move to Port Allen on Kauai's west side, a long haul from the Na Pali.

Cayetano won (Lingle would come back four years later and take the governor's office). The activists cheered. Kusaka seethed.

The payback came in 2002 when Kusaka pulled a plug of her own on the activists, knocking them off of island-wide television.

It's also likely Kusaka had not forgotten the County Council had taken away her new car the year before. The Council members, every bit as much as the activists, basked in the free notoriety they received from the weekly meeting television broadcasts.

Taking away the free publicity medium favored by both the Council and the activists may well have crossed the vindictive mayor's mind.

The activists had long ago figured out that the televised Council meetings gave them a perfect platform from which to hammer county government. It was watched by a huge audience, and, best of all, it was free.

All they had to do was stand up and speak.

Kusaka was fed up with the *haole* activists and their constant carping about her administration. It was time for getting even. "Punish your enemies" is a part of Rule #1 for Kauai politicians.

So, Kusaka shut down the live Hoike telecasts of the Council meetings (but not, of course, her own weekly show).

One fine day in the spring of 2002, Kusaka decreed that airing the Council meetings without closed captioning for the hearing-impaired was a violation of federal law.

Kusaka said that her ever-vigilant County Attorney's Office had decided showing the meetings without closed captioning for the hearing impaired was not allowed by the Americans with Disabilities Act (ADA).

As a result, Council meetings (including the activist antics that infuriated Kusaka) weren't shown until they could be transcribed and captioning provided. That took about a week, which meant they aired *after* the next weekly Council meeting. They were always at least a week behind.

As a source of information for the public and a stage for the activists, the televised meetings had become useless. No one was watching.

The odd thing was that there was no record of any complaints from anyone of an ADA violation.

Not from the deaf community on Kauai. Not from the agencies enforcing the ADA: The State Disability and

Communications Access Board, the U.S. Justice Department, or even the county's own ADA coordinator.

None.

And Kusaka was not particularly a champion of the disabled.

According to some of those who were present, at one cabinet meeting Kusaka went into a tirade about the ADA and how much it was costing Kauai County to provide facilities for the disabled.

Her tantrum was so vicious that her loyal press secretary, Beth Tokioka, left the meeting in tears. Tokioka has a son who is deaf.

Another very strange thing was the Mayor's Office (actually Tokioka) administered the county's contract with Hoike to air the County Council meetings. In all the other counties, it was the county clerk, who works for the County Council rather than the mayor, who handled the television contracts.

Initially, Hoike, a private non-profit agency, refused to shut down the live broadcasts. It announced it would still show them live and then show the meetings with subtitles if and when they became available.

Tokioka told Hoike that the county (meaning the mayor's office) owns and controls the use of all the tapes of County Council meetings.

Tokioka, as she often did, was blowing smoke. The contract did not say the county owns the tapes.

Tokioka continued to lie when she said the mayor's actions shutting down the broadcast were the result of a demand from the State Disability and Communications Access Board.

What really happened was Kauai County asked the state agency whether closed-captioning was required on broadcasts of all government meetings. Kauai County was the one that brought up the topic.

The state responded, in writing, that there was no such requirement for closed captioning broadcasts of government meetings.

Generally, the state Disabilities Board told Kauai County officials, it supported Kusaka's move to require subtitles. But no law requires closed captioning, their letter clearly stated.

Then the *Alice-in Wonderland* character of Kauai County government kicked in: Reality is what Kauai County says it is, not what the law states.

When all else fails, the Kauai County Attorney's Office states that whatever the mayor does is legal, whether it actually is or not.

Once again, no one had the funding to fight the county in court. So Tokioka said the call had been made by the county attorney.

Game over.

Actually, Olelo, the public access cable channel in Honolulu and thus the biggest in Hawaii, did not provide closed captioning of government meetings. And no government agency or individual complained.

The rest of Hawaii recognized there would be a conflict of the "separation of powers" doctrine if the executive branch had control of the legislative branch's television contracts.

Constitutional niceties such as "separation of powers" rarely, if ever, occur to anyone in Kauai government, or at least in the Mayor's Office.

Kusaka blurted out her real motive for yanking the meetings from television on her weekly radio interview when she decided to depart from Tokioka's prepared script and ad-lib.

In one especially candid moment, Tokioka once told a reporter: "I write the scripts but I usually have no idea what's going to come out of her mouth."

One of the noisiest activists, Andy Parks, brought a tape of Kusaka's broadcast outburst to play for the County Council in June 2002.

First, he pointed out, correctly, that there is no legal requirement to delay broadcasts of the Council meetings until closed captioning can be added.

"It does not exist. It's not true. It's a lie," Parks told the Council.

Then he pushed the "play" button on his tape recorder and there was the mayor's voice:

"All the garbage that goes on at the Council meetings—it's such a waste of money paying for it. We allow everybody, and they come to have free rein out there," Kusaka insisted.

Kusaka clearly indicated she would do anything to stop "wasting money" on televising Council meetings because "my critics" were using the meetings as a public forum.

Eventually, the Hoike mess was sorted out. The county contracted with a court-reporting service to provide real-time captioning and the Council meetings were back to being shown live.

The resolution was not the result of a sudden thaw in the frosty relationship between the mayor and the activists (or the mayor and the hearing impaired).

The fact is, 2002 was an election year for the Council. As a means of gaining taxpayer-funded campaign publicity, the incumbents wanted the free air time the televised session gave them, With the long delay waiting for captioning, no one was watching them on TV.

And, as the mayor's radio broadcast revealed, it wasn't about deaf people at all.

It was about those *haoles* who criticized her on island-wide television every week.

Forty years after the enactment of the Civil Rights Act, it's hard for people from the mainland United States—even people in other parts of Hawaii—to realize that, on Kauai at least, it's always all about race.

But it is.

The problem is even more acute in the KPD.

When George Freitas became chief in 1995, he didn't exactly inherit a well-oiled, racially diverse law enforcement machine from former Chief Cal Fujita, who retired under fire.

Far from it.

Fujita's racist hiring practices led to a discrimination lawsuit that eventually cost county taxpayers a bundle and Fujita his job.

Freitas was hired to clean up the mess Fujita had made.

Freitas was given a mandate by the Police Commission (again, the majority appointed by the liberal but by then deposed Mayor Yukimura) to attain and maintain a high standard of diversity within the KPD.

Freitas was the only white member of the department above the rank of sergeant (Freitas is Portuguese, which is considered "local" in Hawaii even if the US Department of Labor counts him as a Caucasian).

But in the Kauai scheme of ethnicity, Freitas, even though born and raised on Oahu, still was an outsider, a *haole*.

Freitas had spent his entire career as a police officer and administrator in Richmond, a very rough suburb of Oakland,

Calif. He didn't speak Pidgin and he didn't share the racial prejudices of most KPD's middle management who had ascended under Fujita's regime.

When Freitas became chief, only two KPD officers were Chinese and only five were women.

KPD officers traditionally were males who had either Japanese or mixed Hawaiian blood.

The KPD has had only one African-American officer in the department's history. And he quit and went to work for the Kauai Fire Department after a very short time.

"There's nothing wrong with the racial mix. We've got a great bunch of cops," said longtime Police Commission Chairwoman Dede Wilhelm in a 2001 interview.

Wilhelm said she went to Kauai's high schools to talk up a police career for young women, "but the wahine don't sign up. It's not glamorous enough."

As for KPD having only two Chinese-American officers, she said: "The Chinese are smart. They go study medicine."

During Kusaka's eight years in office, the word "diverslty" never came up. To the contrary, her press secretary, Tokioka, insisted: "It's the mayor's job to find government jobs for Kauai residents."

A few months after she had left office, it was revealed that Kusaka (or "Queen Maryanne" as all of the County Council members called her, but not to her face) had purposely ignored a new state law aimed at filling a desperate need by all police departments throughout Hawaii for new recruits.

The statute went into effect in July 2002.

For the first time, police departments in Hawaii were allowed to recruit on the mainland. It gave the mayor of every county the power to waive the one-year Hawaii residency requirement for police recruits.

Not only did the mayor of Kauai refuse to use the law, she ordered the County Attorney's Office not to mention it to the Kauai Police Commission.

"As far as I know, there is still a one-year residency requirement," Stanton Pa, then Police Commission Chairman, said seven months after the law went into effect.

Told about the change, he shook his head and sighed, "It's news to me."

Freitas said that despite the fact the KPD had more vacancies than at any time in its entire history—20 of 140 positions went unfilled in 2002—Kusaka repeatedly refused to recruit on the mainland.

In fact, Freitas said, Kusaka refused to recruit outside Kauai.

Freitas said Kusaka screened all of the police applications and interviewed each candidate herself. "She scrutinized every officer we hired," Freitas said.

One of the curious by-products of KPD and Kusaka racism was in the department's choice of targets at the police pistol range. They certainly didn't go unnoticed by *haole* activists.

The KPD pistol range used large poster-size photographs of rough looking and heavily armed individuals as targets for the cops to practice their pistol marksmanship.

Every one of the posters was a blown-up photo of a Caucasian. Not one of the police targets showed a picture of any Asian or Pacific Islander criminals or, for that matter, anyone of color.

Kusaka finally ran up against term limits (two four-year terms) and had to step down. When she tried to extend her political career, she failed.

In 2004, Kusaka ran for state senate and was soundly defeated by Gary Hooser, a former member of the Kauai County Council, a vocal critic of Kusaka's (Hooser was the one who pointed out her lease of a luxury car)

Despite Kusaka's rather shaky ethical record, the election wasn't about ethics because Hooser's were as bad as Kusaka's.

It was revealed during the campaign that Hooser had neglected to pay state withholding and excise taxes he collected from his employees at his magazine publishing company over an 11 year period.

Eventually, the state forced Hooser to repay the $89,875 in taxes but in a deal Hooser cut with the tax collectors, they dropped any penalty or interest, which totaled another $50,440.

The Kauai voters forgave Hooser for cheating the state (and them) out of the penalties and interest.

Hooser was elected. Kusaka was defeated.

Clearly, Kusaka had worn out her welcome with the voters.

. . .

CHAPTER 6: LISA FISHER

After being bludgeoned by the police union and local politicians in his first attempt at imposing discipline in the Monica Alves case, KPD Chief Freitas flinched quite visibly when it next came to dealing with sexual harassment.

Freitas's actions hardly reflected a profile in courage.

When a woman KPD officer was sexually abused by male KPD officers at a KPD station, Freitas punished the victim instead of the perpetrators.

As of last count, KPD has five women officers. That's 3.6 percent of the total force of 140 sworn officers.

The national average for all police departments is 15 percent women, according to *Police Chief Magazine*. In Albuquerque, N.M. and Tucson, Ariz., women officers comprise one-third of the force and in San Jose, Calif., half of the city's police officers are women.

One of the reasons the KPD receives so few applications from women is because of what happened to Lisa Fisher.

Fisher, a Kauai High School alum who grew up dreaming only of being a Kauai police officer, resigned in 1997 because of what she termed "a hostile work environment."

In a lawsuit she filed the following year, Fisher claimed her supervisor at the KPD Hanalei Substation on Kauai's north shore, Sgt. Cecil Baliaris, had repeatedly made suggestions about her body and his genitals, leading other officers to do the same.

Ultimately, Fisher alleged, Officer Michael Kiyabu grabbed her breasts in the police station in front of the other officers.

When she filed a complaint with Freitas, she was taken off the road and given a desk job.

The charges never were investigated, her lawsuit claimed. Although her lawsuit never went to trial, it's quite obvious Fisher was correct.

In 2000, Kauai County paid $425,000 to Fisher to settle the case, not counting the considerable but undisclosed amount it cost the county attorney to hire outside counsel to help the county lose the case.

It was the highest settlement in Kauai history, by far eclipsing Monica Aves's $250,000 settlement and pushing the taxpayer's tab for KPD misconduct even higher.

It also was the first time a woman Kauai County employee ever had sued the county for sexual harassment and discrimination.

It is instructive to note that, even before she won her settlement, Fisher moved permanently to the mainland. She saw no future for herself on the Garden Island.

"As far as I know, no one was ever disciplined in this case," said Richard Wilson, Fisher's Kauai-born Honolulu lawyer.

A lack of oversight that permits questionable racial and gender attitudes is compounded, Wilson asserted, by Kauai's detachment from the rest of Hawaii.

"Kauai is 560 square miles of island located 100 miles from any outside authority," he said. "Kauai is very much the 'Separate Kingdom' it prides itself on, just as its police force is the best example."

. . .

CHAPTER 7: ELAINE SCHAEFER

In another highly-publicized case involving a woman victim, Freitas again sat on his hands while his department did nothing.

Freitas's role as a reformer and his credibility was being rapidly diminished by his own inaction in blatantly obvious cases of police discrimination.

Elaine Schaefer was not a Kauai cop but she was a cop. She was a white retired Oakland police sergeant who had moved to Kauai.

Oakland is a tough town and Schaefer was a tough cop. But the sexist and racist culture within the KPD was even tougher.

One day in May 2000, Schaefer was riding her horse on a secluded North Shore trail with a spectacular view of the open ocean that stretches all the way to Alaska.

Three pit bulls attacked the horse. Schaefer was thrown, and the terrified riderless horse plunged over a cliff and was killed.

Another white woman saw the attack on Schaefer and her horse and spotted a local man who had been hunting with the dogs. Wild pig hunting with dogs is popular with Kauai locals.

As the man ran past her carrying a rifle, he told the witness, "I'm not going to take the blame for this."

The witness provided a KPD artist a description that was turned into a sketch that was published in the Garden Island newspaper.

The KPD was flooded with phone calls from north shore residents, all naming the same individual.

The police report categorized the attack—which should have been written up as reckless endangerment and criminal property damage—as a leash law violation, a petty misdemeanor.

The suspect—who apparently had killed the dogs and hidden their bodies—never was arrested.

There never was a lineup so the witness could try to identify the suspect in person while her memory was fresh.

Eventually, the witness moved back to the mainland.

Three months after the incident, the KPD mailed a driver's license photo of the suspect to the witness. She was unable to pick him out of the photo lineup.

In September 2000, Detective Lt. Glenn Morita, who had been assigned to investigate the case, called Schaefer and told her he had done all he could do and the case was closed. No one would be charged.

Also in September 2000, Detective Lt. Glenn Morita was named "Officer of the Month" by the Kauai Police Commission.

"The minute the sketch of the suspect appeared in the newspaper, everyone on the North Shore knew exactly who it was, but he hasn't been arrested and probably never will be," said a third-generation resident of Kauai.

"Here's a local guy with very close ties to the Kauai Police Department. The victim is a *haole* from the mainland. That's how it is with KPD. That's how it is on Kauai."

• • •

CHAPTER 8: THE SERIAL KILLER

In the spring and summer of 2000 on Kauai's west side, three white women were stabbed and sexually assaulted. Two died. The third was left for dead and so severely injured that it took her three hours to crawl to a telephone only a few yards away and call for help.

It was the first time in recorded history that Kauai had a serial killer on the island.

KPD detectives quickly identified a prime suspect but insisted they could never gather enough evidence to arrest or charge him.

The suspect's brother was a veteran KPD officer.

Property crime and assaults are common but murder is very rare on Kauai. Until the series of killings of women on the west side, there had not been a homicide on Kauai for almost three years.

No detectives on the KPD are designated or trained to investigate murder.

The fact is, in every area of police work, the KPD lacks sophistication in both training and experience.

The KPD runs its own police academy. Many states have a central police academy, usually run by the state police, to provide uniform training to officers from rural departments, but not Hawaii. The popular television series "Hawaii Five-0" is about a state police force that never existed.

The Honolulu Police Department has offered to train "neighbor island" police officers for a set price but Kauai has chosen to remain the "Separate Kingdom" in its police department as in all things governmental.

The primary purpose of the KPD Police Academy is to train new officers in the cultural and political aspects of police work on Kauai, not in law enforcement skills.

The instructors at the KPD Police Academy all are KPD officers. "The blind leading the blind" is an apt description: Poorly trained, unskilled officers teaching raw recruits.

The KPD does send its officers to off-island training courses but there is no guarantee they will attend the classes.

For example, a group of officers recently sent to Maui to be trained in narcotics investigation didn't show up for a single class. They treated the trip as a taxpayer-funded vacation and drinking binge.

So when a major crime occurs on Kauai and there are no obvious suspects, the handling of the cases by the KPD is somewhat less than the stuff of great detective fiction.

If a suspect is a friend or a relative of any KPD officer, the investigation becomes even more like the farcical plot of an Inspector Clouseau movie.

The West Side of Kauai is the most traditional area of the island. It is on the leeward, or *kona* in Hawaiian, side.

Mount Waialeale, termed the spot with the most rainfall on the planet, blocks the trade winds carrying in moisture from the sea to the northeast.

The West side is dry, dusty (red dust from the volcanic soil) and in the summer very hot.

One of two remaining sugar plantations (the other is on Maui) in Hawaii grips the west side of Kauai firmly in the past.

Life is simple. Communities are strong. Native Hawaiians gather salt from an ancient lava field near the surf line. Even the students at Waimea High School are polite to their elders.

On April 7, 2000, the battered body of Lisa Bissell, 38, was found in a roadside ditch near Polihale State Park on Kauai's west side. Polihale is one of Hawaii's most spectacular beaches connected to the rest of Kauai by a web of haul cane roads winding through old sugar cane fields.

Bissell technically lived in Hanapepe where she had a post office box but she was considered a harmless and homeless street person frequently seen in many different towns on the West Shore.

Some of Bissell's belongings were found in a street in Waimea, indicating she had been abducted there.

She was raped, beaten, stabbed. Police said the cause of her death was that her throat had been cut.

Police found an abandoned, bloodstained car. Their theory was Lisa Bissell was killed in one location and her body dumped at Polihale.

On May 22, 2000, a 52-year-old *haole* woman was beaten and stabbed in the yard of a remote Kekaha beach home where she was house-sitting.

The woman never has been identified in the media, although she was well known on Kauai.

Late one night, a year and a half after she was attacked, she called a newspaper reporter at home and gave the only interview she ever has given. A mutual friend convinced her the reporter was trustworthy.

The woman said she was working in the yard of a home she was maintaining for an absentee owner. The house was isolated and right on the beach on the west end of Kekaha.

She said a man walked up to her and said, "My name is John and I'm homeless."

She suggested he go to a house down the beach where the owners often let transients camp on their property.

She turned and went back to work. The man picked her up from behind and took her behind the house where he beat her, breaking one of her arms.

She said he pulled out a knife and stabbed her in the chest but the blade hit her sternum and was bent. The man cursed and threw the knife into some bushes.

She said she believes the only reason her throat was not cut like the two victims who died was that the knife was bent and discarded.

Afterward, she went to the mainland and lived with her family while she recovered.

Months later, KPD flew her to Oahu—not Kauai—where she was shown a lineup. She was able to eliminate two of the men in the lineup but her retinas were detached when she was beaten and her eyesight never was fully restored. She was not able to pick a suspect from the remaining men.

The third victim was found on Aug. 30, 2000, at her camp site near Pakala Point Beach, a popular surfing spot. She was identified as Daren Singer, 43, of Paia, Maui. Paia is a hippie community, much given to alternative lifestyles.

Like the others, she had been sexually assaulted and stabbed. Police said her face was beaten beyond recognition and her throat had been cut.

In each of the three investigations, the first patrol officers on the scene thoroughly contaminated the crime scene by tramping all over any tracks and touching physical evidence.

One of the first things taught in most police academies is that the primary duty of a uniformed officer arriving at a crime scene is to secure the area and protect the evidence so the police technicians will be dealing with an uncontaminated crime scene.

That class apparently is not taught at the KPD Police Academy.

A forensic team flown over from the Honolulu Police Department had almost nothing to work with. DNA evidence, at best, proved "inconclusive."

The KPD had a contract with a mainland lab to conduct DNA testing of evidence. But they went with a lowest bidder that was taking several months to provide results.

It isn't as though the KPD detectives didn't care. If anything, they cared too much. The problem was lack of skills and training and resources.

"One of my biggest concerns when I took this job was the possibility of a serial criminal, a murderer, or a rapist and whether we were equipped to deal with that," said KPD Chief of detectives Lt. Bill Ching, a second-generation Kauai police officer.

"I've seen the resources and manpower serial crimes require and the record-keeping alone is a gigantic task."

Ching's newspaper interview was in itself remarkable. KPD officers in general are not open with the press. Not just because they're cops but also because they're local, and locals don't often share their feelings with *haole* reporters.

The disappointment of West Side residents in their police department had become both obvious and acute.

West Side women repeatedly came into Ching's office and yelled at him for not solving the crimes. Others kept calling him and asking when it would be safe to take walks alone again.

Ching, who has lived his entire life on the West Side, said he and his 10 detectives were taking their inability to arrest anyone very personally. The detectives worked themselves to states of near exhaustion, and many couldn't sleep when they did go home.

"It's hard to step back when some of the people involved are people you've known all your life," Ching noted.

Chief George Freitas attempted to take some of the load off of Ching by forbidding Ching to attend public meetings on the west side with his friends and neighbors. Freitas said he would conduct the meetings.

Ching went to the meetings anyway.

"I told the chief that I didn't want anyone else to have to answer the questions that I was supposed to answer and I went.

"Those community meetings are hard. I reminded people that this is real life, not a television series and nothing is going to be solved in the next hour.

"I had to exercise a lot of control so I didn't give any indication I believed the case was going to be solved in the next day or two, or any indication I believed the case is never going to be solved.

For similar reasons, Ching said he had taken to avoiding friends who are not police officers because they invariably asked him about the investigation.

"It's really hard because I can't say anything."

Ching said he was conducting regular debriefings both with his detectives and west side patrolmen that were as much therapy as police business.

"The first thing I do is let them expose their emotions—good feelings, negative feelings—I let them get it all out. Then we debrief the case itself.

"With these cases I keep reminding them we did everything right. We did everything we were supposed to do. But the waiting for a break is stressful.

"I have two young kids, both in elementary school, and I have to make sure I don't go home and take out my frustrations on them or my wife,

"I was born on the West Side," Ching said. "My mom had 17 brothers and sisters, so I have a lot of relatives holding me accountable for what we were doing. And I have a lot of detectives from the West Side. It's very stressful."

Despite beefed up police patrols and even police horse patrols (with borrowed horses; the KPD doesn't own any) on the beaches, women on Kauai were thoroughly terrified.

KPD and the island's only gun store were deluged with telephone calls from frightened women wanting to buy pepper spray for self defense.

Pepper spray was the weapon the women wanted most but they couldn't get it.

Kauai was the only county in Hawaii to require a permit to carry pepper spray and the ordnance covering it was passed by the County Council at the request of KPD to keep it out of the hands of criminals.

No store on the island stocked pepper spray and the police permit required to carry it required a 14-day waiting period for a criminal background check—the same requirement to buy a handgun.

"A lot of husbands and boyfriends are calling for their wives and significant others," said Emily Fabro, who processed permits for the KPD.

"Personally, I think most women would be better off carrying pepper spray than the short-barrel shotguns they've been buying," said Mike Rosa, co-owner of The Hunting Shop of Kauai.

There is no waiting period on Kauai for purchasing a shotgun. In light of the permit requirement for pepper spray, the logic appears a bit flawed.

Rosa said he didn't carry pepper spray because of the permit requirement and the fact that it has a very short shelf life.

The only other permitted licensed pepper spray dealers were two Kauai police officers who also were licensed gun dealers and they didn't stock it either.

It was a federal violation to ship pepper spray on an airline without declaring it, which appears to be exactly what many Kauaians did.

A thriving black market for the spray developed on Kauai and the demand was met by supplies smuggled in from the other counties where no permit was required.

On Kauai's West Side, where the assaults took place, the three attacks were not something that some women would talk openly about.

"But it's always behind our heads, especially if we go to the beaches or out of the way places, parks," said a woman convenience store clerk in Kekaha. "We stay in groups and use the buddy system."

None of the women ever worked alone without a male co-worker present in the store, which is open evenings, she said.

Billi Smith, the popular and charismatic principal of Kekaha Elementary School on Kauai's West Side, said the school's students had many questions and she and her teachers didn't duck any of them.

Men who lived on the West Side were pondering it, too.

"When I'm working it doesn't cross my mind," said a Kauai firefighter.

"But when I go home and sit down and think about it, it really bothers me.

"Somewhere on this small island is someone who is very capable of very violent attacks on women and it's probably someone many of us see every day."

In early September, KPD detectives rounded up all 70 registered sex offenders on the island. They said they didn't find any suspects but, of course, they had.

On Sept. 12, 2000, the KPD announced it had arrested a convicted rapist on a parole violation. The man's name and mug shot were released through the mayor's office.

The press release was almost instantly followed by another insisting the parole violator was in no way a suspect in the west side attacks and his only crime was violating the conditions of his parole.

The KPD was so vehement in pointing out that the man was *not* the serial killer, every editor in the state bought it.

Except for one Honolulu television station, which used his name and broadcast his picture, all the "news executives" were frightened by the KPD's threat of libel suits.

The next day, the KPD, through the mayor's office criticized the lone television station that identified the arrested man for "irresponsible reporting."

The television station was correct. It was the KPD that was lying. And the mayor's office knew it but lying to the press was pretty much standard operating procedure.

Next, Inspector Mel Morris, head of the investigations bureau, began dragging a red herring claiming, "KPD has not ruled out the possibility that there may be more than one person responsible."

He said the man arrested is "unrelated to any of these cases. Any impression that might have been given that these cases are close to being solved is flat-out wrong."

The arrested man was, of course, KPD's primary, in fact only, suspect and (off the record, of course) they were certain he was the killer but they couldn't prove it.

His name was Waldorf "Wally" Wilson, and his name and picture were all over the west side on anonymously printed flyers.

But the Honolulu media executives would not publish his name until two years later—and then only because Wilson filed a lawsuit against KPD, a newspaper and a magazine.

Wilson was convicted in 1983 of a brutal rape on Oahu. He was paroled on Jan. 9, 1999 and in January 2000 moved to Kauai. The attacks began three months later.

Wally Wilson's brother was a KPD officer, Buddy Wilson, a long-time member of the Vice Squad known for his somewhat less than subtle tactics in investigating narcotics cases.

(Once again the circle that began with the Randy Machado trial looped back. Kelly Lau was a witness for Machado at his trial. Lau indicated quite clearly she was a confidential informant working for Buddy Wilson.)

All the while, KPD insisted Wally Wilson was not a suspect. For the next two years, the KPD engaged in tactics that Wally Wilson later claimed in his lawsuit violated his Constitutional rights.

But he was kept off the streets without ever actually being charged with any crime.

And there were no more attacks.

According to Wally Wilson's lawsuit, KPD "coerced" him into taking a polygraph test on Sept. 12, 2000 and then "strongly pressured" the Hawaii Parole Authority to revoke Wilson's parole. The results of the polygraph test were not given in the lawsuit.

A judge ultimately threw out Wilson's lawsuit but by then KPD's tactics were pretty obvious, as was its complete inability (or unwillingness) to bring criminal charges against him involving the three attacks.

Initially, Wilson's parole was rescinded because he had been in contact with a woman on Kauai that his parole conditions specifically directed him to avoid. The revocation lasted until Feb. 28, 2002, when he was set free.

On June 15, 2002, Wilson was again sent back to prison for violating his parole by failing a polygraph test.

To this day, KPD never has stated Wilson was a suspect at all in the West Side attacks. Yet every time he was released, his parole was violated on one technicality or another, and he was sent back to prison.

The problem is, Wilson has now "maxed out," served the full term for his earlier conviction, and is back on the street. Since he no longer is on parole, he can't be hauled in for parole violations.

The case of the one and only serial killer in Kauai's history remains unsolved.

• • •

CHAPTER 9: OFFICER NELSON GABRIEL

It's impossible to tell the story of the lengthy campaign by Mayor Maryanne Kusaka and the middle management in KPD to oust Chief George Freitas without first understanding the strange case of Officer Nelson Gabriel.

Gabriel was a KPD officer. In 1999, he was indicted on 22 felony charges stemming from the alleged sexual assault of his teenage step-daughter between May 1998 and April 1999.

He was not tried until two years later in October 2001. The right to a speedy trial is guaranteed by the Sixth Amendment to the U.S. Constitution and Rule 48 of the Hawaii criminal court procedures but it often appears that no one on Kauai ever actually has read the U.S. Constitution.

The verdict (issued by Circuit Judge George Masuoka— Gabriel had waived his right to a jury trial) was not rendered until January 2002. Gabriel was acquitted three months after his trial ended and almost three years after he was indicted.

Masuoka said he delayed his ruling because he didn't want to influence the outcome of the investigation into charges against Freitas that was in progress over at the Kauai Police Commission. The accusations against Freitas, which ultimately proved to be a farce, directly involved the Nelson Gabriel trial.

But, in the end, Freitas, who fought to keep his department from violating Gabriel's rights, ultimately lost his job as a direct result of the verdict in Gabriel's trial.

The investigating officer in the allegations against Gabriel was Lt. Alvin Seto. It was Seto and his supervisor, Inspector Melvin Morris, who filed complaints against Freitas.

Seto and Morris were among the KPD middle management digging in its heels every time Freitas moved to modernize KPD.

When Gabriel was indicted and while he was awaiting trial, he was taken off the road and given a desk job in the dispatcher's office located in a rented office almost a mile away from police headquarters.

While he was working at the dispatch office, one of the women dispatchers, annoyed by too much attention from Gabriel, asked for a transfer to a different shift.

At first, she did not file a complaint against Gabriel.

But Lt. Seto pressured her until she did.

Seto later said in an interview that he had "run into the dispatcher's mother in a bookstore and advised her that her daughter could file a formal complaint."

Seto insisted he did nothing beyond that to convince the dispatcher to file a complaint against Gabriel.

But that isn't the way the dispatcher remembered it when she filed her lawsuit against Seto and the County of Kauai.

She said her supervisor went to Seto—who worked in the Investigations Division and had no role or responsibility in dispatcher operations—and told Seto about her request for a shift change.

The supervisor knew Seto was the investigating officer in the molestation case against Gabriel.

"Lt. Seto, in turn, contacted my mother and began pressuring her to pressure me to file criminal charges against Mr. Gabriel," the dispatcher said in her civil complaint.

"Seto was not even supposed to have known about my administrative complaint," she added.

Seto sent two detectives to the dispatcher's father's house (her father was a retired KPD officer and a friend of Seto's) to obtain a formal complaint from her. They also set up a recorded conversation between the dispatcher and Gabriel in hopes Gabriel would say something incriminating.

According to court documents, Gabriel made some admissions that were taped but exactly what he said never was specified in the record and they fell far short of a confession that could be used in court.

The dispatcher said in her lawsuit she was annoyed by Gabriel's attentions.

But she was terrified by Seto's threats.

"At this point, I was afraid to resist the detectives. I was afraid that I would be fired or otherwise disciplined if

I did not now fully yield to the criminal investigation," the dispatcher wrote.

She also said Seto had urged her to lie to the detectives, but she refused to do so.

"Lt. Seto urged me to tell the detectives that Nelson Gabriel had kissed me on my neck at work. He stated: 'Make sure you tell them about Gabriel kissing your neck.'

"The problem was that Nelson Gabriel had never kissed my neck, and I had never stated that he had done so," she said.

"Being pressured to lie in a criminal case by a powerful uniformed man was a terrifying proposition. I did not lie in my statement to the detectives; however, I became sickened with anxiety," she wrote.

The harassment charges involving the dispatcher were misdemeanors and they weren't immediately pursued. They just remained in Seto's back pocket.

Gabriel's trial on the charges of sexually assaulting his step-daughter was rapidly approaching.

Seto was aware that Gabriel's wife planned to testify on her husband's behalf, telling the court her daughter had a long history of being a chronic liar and that she had frequently falsely accused others with whom she became angry of molesting her.

According to court documents in a series of lawsuits filed later, Seto planned to try to force Gabriel's wife to testify against her husband in the molestation case.

If Gabriel's wife did not cooperate and testify for the prosecution instead of her husband, Seto planned to play her the police-taped conversation between the dispatcher and Gabriel.

Seto believed that tape would make Mrs. Gabriel angry at her husband and she would testify against him in his trial.

Seto went to the County Prosecutor's Office and asked the attorney handling Gabriel's case to send a request to the KPD asking that a detective again interview Mrs. Gabriel who, through her lawyer, already had refused to talk to them.

Seto intended to be the detective conducting the interview of Mrs. Gabriel.

All interdepartmental requests cross the police chief's desk and when Freitas saw the request from the Prosecutor's Office, he refused to forward it to Seto.

"A sexual harassment complaint is, by law, totally confidential," Freitas later said.

"If I allowed Seto to try to use a confidential harassment complaint in an attempt to coerce Mrs. Gabriel to change her testimony, the whole effort would be blatantly illegal. I wasn't about to allow that."

Freitas cleared his decision to block Seto's use of the tape with the County Attorney's Office.

The same County Attorney's Office later advised the mayor and Kauai Police Commission to punish Freitas for exactly the action they told him was legal.

Unable to use the tape to sway Mrs. Gabriel, Seto went shopping for a way to retaliate against Chief Freitas.

Seto first attempted to convince the County Prosecutor's Office to charge the police chief with interfering with a police investigation. The prosecutors told him there was no basis for such a charge.

Seto and his boss Morris then went to Mayor Maryanne Kusaka and the Kauai Police Commission and filed a list of charges against Freitas.

The most serious charge was "hindering prosecution" of Gabriel, the same charge the lawyers at the prosecutor's office refused to pursue.

Seto found an attentive audience. The mayor had never supported Freitas. The police commissioners who hired him were long gone, replaced now by Kusaka's appointees.

Meanwhile, the trial of Nelson Gabriel began and a parade of witnesses, including her teachers, testified his step-daughter was a chronic liar. Over a period of years she had accused a number of men with whom she was angry, including her grandfather, of molesting her.

She also lied about a burglary that never took place in an attempt to cover up some damage she had caused at home.

Seto's attempt to blackmail Mrs. Gabriel to testify against her husband blew up in Seto's face.

Michael Green, Gabriel's Honolulu-based attorney, told Seto that if he took the stand he would be cross-examined about his efforts to coerce a witness: Mrs. Gabriel.

Seto decided not to testify. He was not seen again in the courtroom.

It is almost unheard of for an investigating officer to not testify about the evidence he obtained in a criminal case.

No one explained his decision—made just minutes before he was scheduled to take the stand—but no one had to. Everyone on the island knew the true story.

Just as interesting was what was going on out in the audience.

Every day of the trial, Elizabeth Goynes, who was both the police chief's fiancé and a retired Richmond (Calif.) Police Department detective, was in the audience, and she purposely sat behind Gabriel's defense table as sign of support.

Also every day, a group of KPD plain clothes detectives appeared in the audience. They all hugged Goynes and sat with her behind Gabriel.

"This whole case is absolute bullshit," one of the detectives said outside the courtroom. "I don't know what that moron (Seto) is doing because those charges against Gabriel never should have been filed."

Gabriel was acquitted of the 22 felony counts of molesting his step-daughter.

A misdemeanor harassment charge was filed against Gabriel in the case involving the dispatcher. He was given probation and put back on the road as a KPD patrol officer.

Later, Seto retired from KPD and signed on as a supervisor with the civilian security company contracted to guard the U.S. Navy Pacific Missile Range on Kauai.

Ultimately, the dispatcher settled with Kauai County for $100,000—$86,000 in damages, $11,500 for future psychological counseling and $3,000 to settle a worker's compensation claim.

The Council, as usual, approved the settlement in an executive session, even though it is forbidden by the Open Meeting Law from voting on expenditure of public funds behind closed doors.

Kauai County also didn't announce the settlement until a year after the Council approved it. Under law (except on Kauai), amounts paid out by the government to settle litigation are public record as soon as the legislative body approves them.

The county also refused to reveal how much it paid the private attorney who ultimately lost the case for them (and the taxpayers who paid both the lawyer and the settlement). Those expenditures are supposed to be public record.

But, not a single newspaper or TV or radio station filed any complaints about violations of open meetings and public records laws. And, at the next election, Kauai voters returned to office all Council incumbents seeking another term.

· · ·

CHAPTER 10: GEORGE FREITAS

Mayor Maryanne Kusaka liked to portray herself as a kindly retired school teacher, which she certainly is, although many former students will dispute how kindly she was.

For those not familiar with government in Hawaii, there is no city government, only county government. There are four counties: Hawaii, Maui, Oahu and Kauai.

All of the counties have a "strong mayor" system in which the mayor is the chief executive and runs the administrative branch of the government in a manner similar to the federal government and most state governments. The mayor has veto power and the Council may override the mayor's vetoes.

In most jurisdictions of similar size on the mainland, there is a Council-Manager (or Weak Mayor) form of government in which a professional manager runs the administration and the mayor presides at council meetings and cuts ribbons.

So, a mayor in Hawaii has considerably more power than most mainland mayors.

Another major difference is the Kauai County Charter.

Most city charters on the mainland are the size of a metropolitan phone book and spell out in great detail the powers, duties and limitations of every official. Each procedure for each agency is outlined. The Charter is a "Government for Dummies" manual for city employees.

The Kauai County Charter is barely more than a pamphlet. The wording is purposely general and purposely vague. The County Attorney's Office enjoys more than ample wiggle room to interpret it in a way guaranteed to please the incumbent mayor and County Council.

"I like a county charter without a lot of detail. The charter we have gives me a lot of flexibility," said Bryan Baptiste (Kusaka's protégé who replaced her as mayor).

It certainly does. Although a few holes in the charter were patched in the 2006 elections, the whole document is in need of a complete rewrite and major expansion.

Among the many vague sections of the Kauai County Charter is the part covering the removal of the police chief. It's quite clear the chief is hired and fired by the Police Commission, which is appointed by the mayor.

In short, the mayor is not the police chief's boss. The Police Commission is. And that is a galling fact to an insecure mayor (like both Kusaka and Baptiste) who insists on absolute control of all facets of government.

One of the many things unclear in the Kauai County Charter is a provision that states the police chief only can be removed "for cause."

The Charter never defines the term "cause."

Does "cause" mean commission of a felony? Commission of a misdemeanor? Giving his girlfriend a ride in his police car?

The Kauai Charter doesn't say. The charters of all the other counties do.

The definition of "cause" is left entirely up to the county attorney, who is appointed by the mayor, and who, first and foremost, is a hired gun for the mayor.

The county attorney always says what the mayor does is legal, even if it's not.

So, ultimately, the mayor decides.

This brings us to Kauai Police Chief George Freitas, the first police chief in the history of Kauai who was not born and raised on Kauai.

It is impossible to overstate how important it is in Kauai culture to be a native of the island. Anyone who comes from the outside is considered by locals to be taking a job that should have gone to a native Kauaian (even if no one from Kauai is qualified for the job).

Whether Freitas saw the trap he was walking into when he took the job is not clear. But, certainly, Freitas appeared on the scene as an outsider in the wrong time and the wrong place.

He was appointed by a lame duck Police Commission (the police commissioners' terms in office are staggered and overlap the term of the mayor) in 1995, Kusaka's first year in office.

The majority of the Police Commission that hired Freitas had been appointed by Mayor JoAnn Yukimura, a liberal and reformer, who had been defeated for re-election in 1994.

George Freitas, an Oahu native who had spent his entire police career in a California police department was hired by the Kauai Police Commision as KPD chief in the wake of a discrimination lawsuit against former Chief Cal Fujita. He never had the support of either the mayor or the Kauai County Council. Mayor Maryanne Kusaka attempted to force Freitas out but failed. Her protege, Mayor Bryan Baptiste finally forced Freitas to resign when the chief finally ran out of money to hire lawyers to fight the county.

George Freitas was hired by a lame duck Police Commission entirely different from the political culture Kusaka brought back to the mayor's office.

Freitas was doomed to failure the first day he pinned on his KPD badge.

Freitas was an outsider who didn't bow down to the mayor.

She hadn't hired him, she couldn't fire him. He didn't work for her, and he didn't much like her.

The loathing was mutual. She had no use for him.

By the time her second (and last due to term limits) term began in 1999, there had been considerable grumbling among the locals in the KPD who comprised middle and upper management and who were not at all keen on being "modernized" by Freitas.

More important in Kusaka's scheme to keep a tight rein on the KPD, the majority of police commissioners were now Kusaka appointees. Freitas's bosses now were Kusaka's cronies.

Freitas had been hired as a reform chief to reverse the racist hiring policies of previous chiefs.

Problem was, both Kusaka and the KPD old guard feared diversity. They weren't anxious for change at all.

Freitas' record, particularly regarding sexual discrimination, was less than spectacular, as pointed out in previous chapters.

What is interesting is that Kusaka did not go after Freitas on that issue, even though he was highly vulnerable.

Perhaps Kusaka didn't recognize discrimination as an issue she could use to rid herself of her less-than-obedient police chief.

Freitas' efforts in adding diversity to the KPD were impressive, especially since Kusaka had pretty much limited Freitas to recruiting only on Kauai.

By 1999, Freitas had recruited a considerable number of Filipinos and even a few white officers and a few women to the KPD. The monopoly of the Hawaiian and Japanese men on the force was beginning to erode.

The power struggle between the chief and at least some of his subordinate supervisors already was underway by the beginning of Kusaka's second term.

Enter Lt. Alvin Seto and Inspector Mel Morris.

When the County Prosecutor's Office refused to press charges on Seto's claim that Freitas had "hindered prosecution" in the Nelson Gabriel case, Seto and his boss, Inspector Mel Morris, began shopping around for a more sympathetic ear.

In late July, 2001, they found an ally in Mayor Maryanne Kusaka. They handed Auntie Maryanne what she believed was the "cause" to get rid of her unwanted *haole* police chief.

She took it straight to her handpicked gang of police commissioners.

It is instructive to note that, from that day forward, with only one exception, Kusaka used her "ex officio" status to attend all of the Police Commission meetings, something she never did before or would do afterward.

In a secret meeting on Aug. 10, the Kauai Police Commission—with Kusaka present—voted to place Freitas on involuntary leave with pay.

Freitas was off island that day. He didn't have a chance to answer the charges. He never would.

Later, Freitas said he probably could have answered all of the Commission's questions if he had been invited to their meeting.

But Kusaka had an ambush in mind.

This was going to be Kusaka's most glorious moment in ethnically cleansing Kauai government of outsiders.

Although it later was brought to her attention that the FBI is the agency with the jurisdiction to investigate state and local government corruption cases, Kusaka's staff said she never considered that option.

Kusaka has no control over the FBI but the police commissioners all were her loyal and grateful appointees, as was the county attorney who was advising the commission.

A month after suspending Freitas, Kauai "borrowed" John Ko, an investigator, from the Honolulu Police Commission.

At taxpayer expense, Ko for two months lived at one of Kauai's most posh resorts, drove an unmarked Kauai police car and interviewed more than 150 KPD officers and civilian employees—pretty much the entire department.

Many of those interviewed said privately that the questions asked by Ko were mostly open-ended and not about specific incidents.

Clearly, Ko was looking for additional charges against Freitas. Just as clearly, he was on a very expensive (to Kauai taxpayers) fishing expedition. Judging from subsequent events, he never even got a nibble.

The county has refused numerous requests to release the files covering the cost to taxpayers of Ko's stay on Kauai.

As usual, the state's news organizations would not pony up for a lawyer to try to pry what should have been public record out of Kauai. Challenging the government and fighting for open meetings and public records is not in the tradition of Hawaii journalism.

Ko produced a report that found nothing new, but he appended to it an enormous stack of interview transcripts that obviously had nothing incriminating in any of them.

Although it really was nothing more than a stage prop for the island-wide television audience, Ko's gigantic but meaningless report sat on the conference table at every Police Commission meeting about Freitas.

It never was opened. No one ever quoted it. But its sheer mass was quite impressive and proof (or at least a hint) that there had been a thorough investigation, even if it found nothing.

Ko's masterpiece also never has been made public despite repeated requests. Hawaii state public records law says the documents related to any investigation are public record once the case is concluded.

Even more amazing, the Police Commission refused to give Freitas a copy of Ko's report or state in writing the charges against him. And that was a violation of the County Charter.

On Nov. 23, 2001, more than three months after he was suspended (a term Kusaka's people repeatedly objected to—"placed on involuntary leave" was what they wanted to see in the newspapers), the Police Commission for the first time publicly unveiled the charges against Freitas and even voted to toss some of them out.

The most serious charge was the "hindering prosecution" complaint involving Gabriel, which in the end proved to be totally bogus.

A lot of jaws dropped in the room when the rest of the list was read aloud:

- That Freitas violated the Americans with Disabilities Act when he brought up a medical condition of an officer (Seto) during a private departmental meeting on officer assignments.

- That Freitas showed disrespect toward an officer (again, Seto) when he hung up on him during a telephone conversation.

- That Freitas improperly transported a civilian (his girlfriend and later wife Elizabeth Goynes, a retired

California police officer) in his unmarked police car for non-police purposes on July 21, 2001.

- That Freitas and Goynes used the unmarked KPD car to house hunt on that date and that, while looking at houses, he parked illegally.

- That on Aug. 2, 2001, a few days after Seto and Morris had filed the complaint against Freitas but before he was suspended, Freitas allegedly had yelled at Morris during a private meeting in Freitas' office, causing Morris to suffer a "nervous breakdown" that required him to take several days off of work.

- That in the same meeting, Freitas had violated Morris's rights by ordering him to keep what they discussed in the meeting confidential.

That was it.

After two months of questioning everyone in the department, that was all Seto and Morris and John Ko and Maryanne Kusaka could come up with.

But, again, there is no definition of "cause" in the County Charter and Kusaka figured she had enough to convince the Police Commission to fire Freitas.

In the meanwhile, Freitas had hired Margery Bronster as his attorney.

During her tenure as Hawaii attorney general, Bronster had prosecuted members of the board of trustees of the

Bishop Trust (the richest trust fund in the world, which was established to educate Native Hawaiians) for fraud. She ranks among Hawaii's "superstar" lawyers.

One of the Kauai Police Commission (aided and abetted, of course, by the County Attorney's Office) tactics was to refuse to announce when Freitas' case was on its agenda for an executive session. State law requires the subject of executive sessions be clearly stated.

This agenda camouflage began to be applied after Freitas waived his right to privacy in Commission proceedings involving him. He wanted the public and press to witness the Commission at work.

But if his name didn't appear on an agenda and no one knew if or when Freitas would be discussed, the public didn't show up.

Reporters, Freitas and Bronster spent a lot of time together in the hallway outside the locked Commission door waiting.

"Is it always like this in Kauai government?" Bronster asked the first time the Commission pulled this stunt.

"Every day," a reporter told her.

Bronster immediately filed a lawsuit in federal court, claiming Kauai County violated Freitas' civil rights (and his rights clearly guaranteed in the County Charter) by suspending him without providing any written charges to him and by failing to conduct a hearing at which he could face his accusers, Seto and Morris.

In his lawsuit, Freitas denied all the accusations against him except one: He admitted he had given Goynes a ride in his police car but denied they had ever used the county car to go shopping for a house.

U.S. District Judge Susan Mollway asked the attorneys for both Freitas and Kauai County for more detailed briefs.

The judge also blocked a hearing the Police Commission had scheduled for Dec. 28 at which Freitas was scheduled to be the only witness. None of his accusers was to testify.

The Police Commission still met, it just didn't conduct a hearing. As usual, Mayor Maryanne Kusaka attended the lengthy executive session. She remained for the public session but did not speak.

At that meeting, the Police Commission voted to drop the charges against Freitas involving allegedly violating the Americans with Disabilities Act, hanging up on Seto, telling Morris to keep the subject of his meeting with Freitas confidential, and illegally parking his police car.

That left the hindering prosecution charge, the giving his fiancé a ride in his police car charge, and the yelling at Morris charge.

Then, on Jan. 2, 2002, Deputy County Attorney Laurel Loo wrote Freitas advising he could return to work the following Monday, even though three charges against him were still pending before the Police Commission.

The Police Commission, which is the only entity that can, under the County Charter, hire and fire and suspend and reinstate a police chief, did not vote to put Freitas back to work. The County Attorney's Office reinstated Freitas without a vote of the Police Commission.

In fact, the commission refused at its previous meeting to consider a request from Freitas that he be allowed to return to work until the case was resolved.

It never has been made clear who made that decision but clearly it was blessed by Kusaka and, just as clearly, the mayor was beginning her retreat.

Freitas went back to work.

Meanwhile, back in federal court, Judge Mollway on Jan. 18, 2002, turned down a request from Kauai County to dismiss Freitas's lawsuit.

The judge took a shot at lawyer Loo's somewhat diminished skills at writing legal briefs and reasoning: "Defendants appear to be asserting (less than clearly) that counties and county officials acting in their official capacities are not 'persons'...and therefore cannot be held liable for claims. That assertion is wrong."

The judge also raised questions about the confidentiality of information in the case: "They (Kauai County's lawyers) do not explain what state or federal law, or what court order, requires them to keep information regarding the charge against Freitas confidential."

In effect, the judge kicked the door open on Kauai's efforts to keep both documents and meetings out of the public eye.

The tiny Kauai press corps cheered the judge's ruling. But their editors just hunkered further down behind their desks.

Once again, no news organization would spend the money to hire a lawyer to pursue the court's favorable inclination.

On Jan. 24, 2002, Judge Masuoka announced his decision that Nelson Gabriel was innocent on all 22 felony counts against him.

Five days later, the Kauai Police Commission resolved all the remaining charges against Freitas.

Masuoka repeatedly had said he would not rule on the Gabriel case until the Police Commission concluded the investigation of Freitas.

When Masuoka ruled a few days *before* the Police Commission acted, it was a clear indication the outcome of the Freitas probe had been decided before the Commission met for a formal vote. There can be no doubt Masuoka was told beforehand what the Commission would decide.

Most important, the Police Commission absolved Freitas of the hindering prosecution charge.

The Commission found Freitas had violated department policy by giving Goynes a ride in his police car and was disrespectful to Inspector Morris (who, along with Seto, had by this time retired from the KPD) by yelling at him during a private meeting in Freitas' office.

The Commission voted to send Freitas two letters of reprimand on the two policy violations.

Freitas, however, was fuming.

The County Charter guarantees a Kauai police chief be given a written statement of the charges against him and receive a hearing before the Police Commission votes.

Freitas had received neither the statement nor the hearing.

"I'd still like to know exactly what I'm supposed to have done so I can answer the complaint," Freitas said. "More than 150 interviews (by investigator John Ko) and this is the best we can do?"

Freitas said the whole matter could have been resolved the previous summer if the Police Commission "had the courage" to show him the complaint and discuss it with him at the outset.

"Who drove this thing?" Freitas asked. "I have no idea."

Of course, Freitas knew. The whole island knew.

Not by accident, this was the only meeting of the Police Commission that Mayor Maryanne Kusaka did not attend since the Freitas affair began.

Clearly, the outcome had been decided before the commissioners ever voted and Kusaka didn't want to be around to witness (or be interviewed by the press about) her own defeat.

Because he was reinstated and lost no pay, Freitas' lawsuit against Kauai County became moot. But it had served its purpose.

Bronster said she was convinced the filing of the lawsuit in federal court by Freitas was the only reason he kept his job. She said she believed the commission records, which still were being kept secret, would "reveal that the plan from the outset was to hunt for an excuse to fire him."

The commission records remain sealed. The news media would not pay for a lawyer to go to court to force Kauai County to make them public.

· · ·

CHAPTER 11: A NEW MAYOR

George Freitas' reinstatement as police chief came early in 2002, the last year of Maryanne Kusaka's term as mayor.

By 2002, Kusaka was very much a lame duck and had little incentive to reopen her war with the chief. She left it to her successor to try again to get rid of Freitas.

Bryan Baptiste, a member of the County Council and Maryanne Kusaka's protégé, was elected mayor in the fall of 2002. He was known in some circles (not very flatteringly) as "Son of Kusaka."

Baptiste was so accomplished at fleecing Kauai taxpayers that he managed one last grab at the public coffers even in death.

After Baptiste died following heart surgery in June 2008, his cabinet put on a huge memorial service at the Kauai Convention Center.

The county paid overtime for drivers and fuel costs for special buses to collect anyone anywhere on the island who wanted to attend. Additional buses were added to ferry mourners from a nearby parking lot to the convention center.

Obviously, there was no money for a "state funeral" in the county's budget, the costs were not made public and the Council never approved the funding beforehand.

Baptiste's cronies simply spent the tax dollars without approval from anyone.

Baptiste won Kusaka's favor while he was on the County Council. He volunteered to head one of her pet projects: The beautification of the entrance to Lihue Airport.

Never mind the fact that Lihue Airport was a state airport and the entrance was on a state highway and maybe the state, not Kauai County, should have paid for it.

Baptiste rounded up a large roster of clubs and organizations. Each "adopted" an area of the project with a promise of perpetual care.

When completed, the area, formerly fallow cane fields, had been transformed into a beautiful garden. Signs welcomed tourists driving out of the airport when they arrived and thanked tourists entering the airport when they departed.

On Kauai, tourists are indeed the geese that lay golden eggs.

But the "perpetual care" didn't last long.

AMFAC (long ago shortened from American Factors and then bought by a real estate company in Chicago), the one-time huge sugar plantation that had promised to provide free water for the flowers, went out of business.

The clubs soon ignored the project and the gardens started to become tangled masses of weeds.

When he became mayor, Baptiste put county work crews to work repairing and maintaining the project. No one mentioned the "volunteerism" that vanished or the fact the county taxpayers were stuck with the maintenance bill.

Kusaka didn't publicly endorse Baptiste as her choice for the next mayor until late in the campaign.

But that was all for show. The same business interests that backed Kusaka had found their new puppet in Baptiste and were pouring money into his coffers.

Largely thanks to what he claimed was a sizable last-minute "loan" from a wealthy relative on Oahu, Baptiste was able to launch a media blitz in the final weeks of the campaign.

The roadsides of Kauai were blanketed with placards promoting "Honest Bryan Baptiste."

Baptiste narrowly defeated long-time Council Chairman Ron Kouchi, easily the brightest and most politically intuitive politician on Kauai. Drop a pebble in a pond, and Kouchi could accurately predict where and when every ripple would touch the shore.

The early favorite, Kouchi's greatest strength, his intellect, also was his Achilles' heel. In the eyes of Kauai locals who pride themselves on their very minimal education, Kouchi was "scary smart."

He operated on a level most locals couldn't comprehend (he used a lot of big words) and hinted at support for changes. Kouchi became a potential threat to the "Kauai Style" that true locals want to remain forever fixed.

Kouchi, a member of the wealthy family that owned and operated Kauai's largest private waste disposal company, exuded more than a little arrogance.

He was and remains an elitist. In an Asian culture in which perceived humility is the greatest virtue, Kouchi's lack of appropriate modesty fatally flawed his campaign for mayor.

Exhibit A: Rarely would anyone come up and hug Ron Kouchi.

Exhibit B: Everyone hugged Bryan Baptiste.

Shaped somewhat like a brown Pillsbury Doughboy, bald and with a wispy mustache, Baptiste appeared not the least bit threatening: The very portrait of a benign despot, a Kauai local's dream leader.

The fact that he was not terribly bright or articulate actually was a political plus on Kauai. He was an "everyman," the candidate most like the voters.

And he had a political pedigree.

Baptiste's father, Tony Baptiste, had been chairman of the county board of supervisors in the 1950s and '60s, before the counties all switched to a municipal form of government. In effect, he was the equivalent of the mayor.

Tony Baptiste ran Kauai County from a jail cell for a year while serving a term for tax evasion, and that says a great deal about the forgiving nature of the Kauai electorate.

"The voters were so angry at him, they only re-elected him three more times," Bryan Baptiste liked to point out.

That boast says a whole lot more about Bryan Baptiste and his lack of a moral compass than it does about his father.

As long as the voters love you, it doesn't matter how crooked you are. That was the mindset Baptiste carried into the mayor's office.

Like Kusaka, who became a Republican to run for mayor in the 1994 primary, Baptiste was a Democrat who turned Republican.

RINO (Republican In Name Only) is what both Kusaka and Baptiste were called.

Just as Kauai County government is almost exclusively a brown-skinned club, a conclave of Kauai Republicans is a vast sea of white faces drinking punch and eating cookies in a resort conference room.

Many were members of the Navy League (which won them free joyrides on Navy ships), and it was this constituency retired Capt. Bob Mullins had brought to Kusaka's front door. When Mullins left to sell military hardware, they remained true to Kusaka and later to Baptiste.

Kusaka and Baptiste certainly looked out of place in the great *haole* herd but they got what they wanted: The GOP faithful believed each of the mayors were one of them. No need to look any further.

Events would prove exactly the opposite was true, but that "R" behind a politician's name carries a lot of weight in the wealthy retirement communities of Princeville and Poipu.

Baptiste's conversion came after Kusaka gave him the job of managing the county's convention center, a large meeting facility that never actually hosted a major convention. Many people who went to the convention center mistook Baptiste for the janitor.

And so, Baptiste became a Republican.

"The mayor was a Republican, so switching parties when I took the job just seemed the polite thing to do," Baptiste said.

Baptiste was hardly a true believer in the GOP. Nor was he philosophically a true Democrat.

The longer Baptiste served as mayor, the more it seemed he became convinced he had been chosen to rule by "Divine Right."

It didn't hurt him at all that Republican Linda Lingle had just become the first GOP governor of Hawaii since the 1960s in the same election in which Baptiste became Republican mayor of Kauai.

He brought in several new department heads—all of them born on Kauai, although some had migrated to Honolulu and had to be "brought home."

Included was County Attorney Lani Nakazawa, a Stanford classmate of former mayor (now Council Member) JoAnn Yukimura.

Nakazawa brought to the office both a keen intellect and a philosophy that it was the role of an attorney to do anything (and everything) to protect her client, no matter what laws or ethical codes she violated.

And she brought with her a very mean and vindictive spirit that she cloaked behind a benign and constant smile.

Under Nakazawa's guidance, virtually any complaint to the Council or a board or commission instantly became "a possible subject for future litigation." The topic of the complaint thus was forever barred from becoming a matter of public record.

This was true even if the person complaining was simply exerting a First Amendment right and had no intention of filing a lawsuit against the county.

Similarly (although this was true during Kusaka's reign as well), any time a board or commission met in executive session to discuss its powers, duties, liabilities and limitations with the County Attorney (an exemption from the open meetings statutory requirement that appeared on every agenda of every board and commission), the entire meeting was closed and the minutes forever kept secret.

The fact is, usually only a tiny fraction of the meetings involved getting advice from the lawyer (sometimes none of it at all because the lawyer wasn't even in the meeting room).

There is no doubt that most (or all) of the executive sessions consisted of discussions that legally should have been in open session.

Hawaii's Open Meeting Law contains a preamble that states the statute should be "liberally construed" and errors, if they are made, should be in the direction of keeping meetings open to the public.

Give Kusaka's County Attorney Hartwell Blake credit, at least, for honesty. "I construe that statute very conservatively," he explained. He was admitting he was violating the law, or at least its stated intent.

Nakazawa did the same but she was much more devious than Blake.

Nakazawa also introduced a new fad, already popular on the mainland, which sealed records because personal information about private citizens was discussed in executive sessions: "Privacy Rights."

She encouraged members of boards and commissions to toss out a few tidbits of gossip about private individuals so the executive session minutes could be forever sealed because there were "privacy issues" involved.

And she had a sense of humor, of sorts.

Asked whether there was any case law in Hawaii or elsewhere to back up any of her constant advice to the county officials to keep meetings closed and file cabinets locked, her response, given with her trademark smile, was: "Well that's why they're called county attorney's opinions, not county attorney's facts."

Translation: "If you don't like it, sue me."

Nakazawa knew the chances of any journalist or any political activist challenging her methods in court was just about zero.

And, if they did sue, Kauai County has unlimited taxpayer dollars to hire outside lawyers to keep its secrets from public scrutiny.

The County Council repeatedly appropriated sums of $100,000 and more to hire outside legal counsel for her to fight any legal challenges in court. No individual challenger could match the county's war chest and no news editor had the backbone.

The number of executive sessions skyrocketed. The news media editors continued to sit on their hands and their publishers' wallets.

A study by *The Garden Island* newspaper found Kauai County paid $1.9 million to private law firms defending the county and KPD against lawsuits in 2006. That's out of a total county budget of only $122 million.

And In every case but one (the only one that went to trial), Kauai County settled all of the lawsuits against KPD for large sums of taxpayer money.

Rather than risking public trials with the press covering highly embarrassing public testimony of witnesses—including county officials—Kauai County agreed to pay huge sums of money to almost anyone who sued the police department.

• • •

CHAPTER 12: BRYAN BAPTISTE

"The mayor sat there like the Godfather, with his arms folded over his belly, and assured us in no uncertain terms he would make sure the state issued the required permits," said television producer Eric Westmore.

An NBC *Discovery Kids* film crew had arrived on Kauai in June 2004 along with containers filled with expensive rented movie equipment and highly-paid technicians already on the clock to shoot the third season of *Endurance*, a Saturday-morning reality show for kids based not very loosely on *Survivor*.

They believed Mayor Baptiste's film commissioner, Tiffany Lizama, had obtained the location and all the state permits they need to shoot on Kauai.

They believed wrong.

"When we got here, door after door closed in our faces. There were a lot of promises, but very few were delivered on," said JD Roth, the show's creator, producer and host.

Ultimately and very quickly, the very resourceful private sector location manager on Kauai, Angela Tillson, who had guided many other producers, found the show a location and obtained its permits.

Lizama, whom Baptiste had inherited from Mayor Kusaka, chose to resign very shortly afterward.

Lizama worked directly for Beth Tokioka, Mayor Kusaka's former press secretary whom Baptiste had appointed Kauai's economic development director.

Bryan Baptiste was the Kauai mayor who forced out both of the KPD chiefs who were brought in by the Police Commission to reform the department. His ethnic cleansing of all of Kauai government (all of his department heads were either born on Kauai or married to an native Kauaian) made him very poular among locals, who make up about 60 percent of the voters. Yet, when he stood for reelection in 2006, he won by only two votes. Baptiste died following heart surgery in June 2008.

Tokioka previously characterized the film commissioner's job as "nothing more than being a glorified tour guide."

The Kauai Film Commission's 2004 Annual Report, written after a long-time entertainment pro, Art Umezu, was hired to replace Lizama, sugar-coated the whole episode this way:

"Despite numerous challenges associated with the production, the resulting show aired September–October 2004 and provided excellent exposure for Kauai, again on a major network."

But everyone on Kauai knew what a near-train wreck it had been.

It was one of many embarrassments that Baptiste, who didn't have a clue how to run a county government, caused Kauai.

Baptiste hired a press secretary who had absolutely zero experience with either the media or public relations. But she was the daughter of a long-time friend and she needed the work.

She eventually departed but has been replaced by other political hacks, each less qualified than the one before.

It wasn't so much that Baptiste started out with *bad* press relations. He started out with *no* press relations. And it got worse from there.

Baptiste's first major public relations disaster was his decision to use the KPD (which Baptiste, like Kusaka, believed should be his private army) to evict the homeless from the county beach parks and threaten them with jail if they came back.

This was to keep his local constituents (that 60 percent of the population and the voters on Kauai) happy.

Local families make heavy use of the county beach parks on the weekends. They erect elaborate pavilions for shade, haul endless ice chests of beer and food to the public barbecues, and swim and surf, and cast for fish.

They didn't like the homeless squatters, most of them white (on some beaches white hippies, whom locals detest), as neighbors. So, the mayor kicked them out.

Kauai was the only county in Hawaii without a homeless shelter. The Kauai Humane Society boasted a dog pound that cost $3 million donated mostly by Princeville *haoles* to build but there was nothing for people without homes. Rich *haoles* love dogs, not poor people.

The beach parks, obviously, were not designed as homeless shelters, but they gave the homeless places to camp that had electricity, restrooms, showers, running water, and trash collection.

Kauai's homeless are quite different from the mainland bums begging on street corners. Many—including the hippies who worked as farm laborers—held jobs.

But with the median price of a home well above a half million dollars and a serious lack of inexpensive rental units, they just couldn't afford a place to live. So they camped on the county beaches.

One of the benefits of Hawaii's' gentle climate is that a tent is very adequate shelter all year.

Many of the homeless families had children, and the children attended public schools. The school buses stopped at the beach parks to pick them up every morning and brought them home every afternoon.

The social service agencies that provided basic services from a mobile van knew where to find them.

The homeless camps typically were off in one corner of the park. They were clean—the homeless children policed up trash several times a day—and there was very little, if any, crime. They didn't panhandle, and they didn't mingle with other people using the beach parks.

When he announced the eviction of the homeless via press release, Baptiste did not respond to a request for an interview.

His office also did not respond to a request for police reports documenting any criminal activity by the homeless in the parks. In his press release, Baptiste claimed an increase in the amount of crime due to the homeless.

Fern Grotto State Park, which underwent a facelift engineered by Mayor Bryan Baptiste's administration in a method experts say was illegal. The State of Hawaii granted the money to Kauai County with the understanding Kauai would administer the restoration. Kauai then re-granted the money to the Kauai Chamber of Commerce without bothering to tell state officials. Without seeking bids, the Chamber then contracted with one of Baptiste's best friends and closest political allies to do the work, a blatant violation of state procurement law.

Baptiste's claims about the homeless in the parks simply were untrue, said Stephanie Fernandes, homeless and housing director for Kauai Economic Opportunities (KEO), a nonprofit social service agency.

"The police have never come to KEO complaining of any violence or theft in the camping areas. The only complaints I get are from the homeless campers who say local people come to the parks at night, get drunk and try to pick fights with them," she said.

Baptiste's eviction of the homeless (the technical excuse was they didn't have required county camping permits) forced them to move into fallow sugar cane fields with no water or sanitation.

Baptiste promised to build a homeless shelter, and ultimately he sort of did. It was totally inadequate and it took more than three years to complete.

It provides "transitional housing" for 12 families. The estimated number of homeless people on Kauai is more than 600.

Baptiste's experience in administering a county agency was limited to his brief tenure as the Kusaka-appointed manager of the County Convention Center.

In fact, Baptiste, upon taking the oath of office, turned the task of running the government to Gary Heu, formerly the Kauai manager for the Verizon Telephone Company.

Baptiste didn't even know Heu when he offered him the job. All he knew was the telephones on Kauai usually work and Heu was about to be transferred off of Kauai by Verizon and desperately wanted to stay.

Heu is both a highly talented manager and a good soldier. He never reveals his personal feelings on an issue. When Baptiste tells him to do something, he salutes and follows orders.

Heu stayed down in the engine room kept the wheels and gears of county government churning while Baptiste was up on the bridge pretending to steer the ship, which never seemed to arrive at any port.

In his first 12 months in office, Baptiste did not ask the County Council for a single piece of legislation.

The first year, he called only two news conferences, one on his tourism promotion trip to Japan and the other to announce (but not be questioned about) his decision to toss the homeless out of the county parks.

Baptiste's unveiled fear and loathing of reporters was an acknowledgement of his total inability to articulate his positions on issues. It guaranteed him bad notices.

Contrast that with Baptiste's contemporary, Mayor Harry Kim of the Big Island (or, more formally: Hawaii County).

Kim was a master at the care and feeding of reporters.

If a reporter called any department head in Hawaii County, the reporter ended up talking to the mayor. Kim knew the issues and was not afraid to give his views openly.

Harry Kim's press secretary? A retired reporter for Reuters, one of the world's premier news services.

Baptiste was a walking (more often sitting, actually) public relations nightmare.

"I'm not very good at PR," he explained. "I'm not going to publish anything in the paper until it's finished." And he didn't finish anything in that first year.

He did, at times, have a self-effacing sense of humor.

Unlike Kusaka, who circled the globe seeking out tourists, Baptiste refused to take those taxpayer-funded junkets.

"You don't want to see me hula dance," he joked.

Baptiste turned his energies to "listening to the people" at an endless series of Town Hall meetings he created all over the island. He said he would only do what the people told him they wanted him to do at those Ka Leo meetings.

The problem was that Baptiste purposely never announced a project until it was in the bag.

By then, it was too late for public comment.

In his spare time, Baptiste engaged in what his staff characterized as "deep thinking."

Bryan Baptiste started his first term in December 2002 with an inaugural address that didn't give any details of his plan or vision for Kauai County.

He had managed to win election the same way. Despite six years on the Kauai County Council, during his campaign for mayor, Baptiste made no specific statements on the county's affordable housing shortage, traffic jams, filled-to-capacity county dump, and soaring property taxes.

Nothing.

After his first 100 days in office, Baptiste issued himself a "report card" and gave himself straight As. The "report card" included progress on only one of the many issues facing Kauai County: "The War on Drugs." The term was coined 20 years earlier by President Ronald Reagan. Apparently, Baptiste wanted to show he was a "true Republican."

In fact, Baptiste's sole achievement in fighting a huge and growing narcotics problem had been to name a committee to select a coordinator for Drug Czar, a job he ultimately gave to an out-of-work political hack.

The "report card" came in the form of a press release from the mayor's office. He was "not available" for questions after its release.

What Baptiste did best was take care of his political supporters.

Lest no one forget: Rule #1 for the Mayor of Kauai is: "Support your friends, punish your enemies."

Exhibit A is Lelan Nishek, owner of Kauai Nursery and Landscaping.

According to Baptiste's very sketchy biography that he uses for campaigns (none is available at all on the Kauai

County website), Kauai Nursery was Baptiste's only private sector employer. Ever.

After Baptiste became mayor, a terrible calamity took place. The new mayor acted with dispatch and certainty by calling in his old pal Nishek to fix it.

County employees who had been collecting and mulching the green waste on Kauai (and on a jungle island there's an almost unlimited supply of green waste) had broken the county machinery used to grind up all those leaves.

The official version was that the workers failed to sort out the large stones that often are collected with the green waste and thus jammed and eventually broke the machines.

Mayor Baptiste immediately declared an "emergency," which allowed him to award a contract for disposing of green waste without any call for bids. He gave the job to Nishek and Kauai Nursery, saying there was no other company equipped to do the job.

(When Ka Loko Dam burst in 2006 killing seven people, it created an enormous amount of green waste that needed to be collected. The State of Hawaii put the job out for bids and there was no shortage of companies throughout the state willing and capable of doing the job).

Every year, rather than fixing the county equipment and supervising the county workers so they would take the rocks out of the green waste, there was a new "emergency" and Kauai Nursery got a new (and usually higher-priced) no-bid contract.

For each of several years, Nishek was being paid up to $300,000 of taxpayer money and given tons of free shrubbery to make the mulch he then resold at Kauai Nursery. As of 2006, the county has hired a second contractor to process green waste, but only because Nishek couldn't handle it all. Not because it went out for bids.

But wait. There's more.

Exhibit B also is Lelan Nishek and Kauai Nursery and Landscaping.

In 2002, the Hawaii Legislature passed a law requiring the Hawaii Tourism Authority (HTA) to spend at least $1 million (of the roughly $60 million it collects annually in taxes on hotel rooms) to repair state parks and trails.

In 2003, without a "needs study" to guide them (although plenty of "needs studies" had been done on the seriously dilapidated parks system in the past), the HTA went to each of Hawaii's four mayors and allowed each to pick a park or hiking trail on their islands to be the first repaired under the new law.

Bryan Baptiste chose Fern Grotto State Park on the Wailua River.

Fern Grotto is sort of a human-enhanced natural wonder. As the name implies, it is a huge natural grotto, or shallow cavern, 150-feet high, in the side of a limestone cliff right on the riverbank.

In pre-contact (pre-Captain Cook) times, Fern Grotto was used by Hawaiians for ceremonies. The acoustics were close to perfect.

The ferns began growing only after sugar cane was grown on the land above the cave. Plantation workers built a catch basin for storm runoff that became known as Reservoir 21 directly above the cave.

Water from the reservoir percolated through the soil, and a lush growth of maidenhead and Boston ferns 12 to 15 feet long sprouted from the roof of the cavern.

A small waterfall flowing in front of the cave entrance nourished the rich plant life surrounding the entrance to the grotto.

For decades Fern Grotto was a "must see" attraction for visitors. During the 1970s and 1980s, Fern Grotto was visited by 600,000 tourists each year and about 1,000 weddings were conducted there annually.

Eyeing a bountiful revenue flow from what already was state land, Fern Grotto was named a state park.

Two companies, Smith's Boat Services and Waialeale Boat Tours, paid rent to the state for use of the state marina at the mouth of the Wailua River and for use of Fern Grotto State Park.

Actually, what they were paying for was a shared and exclusive concession to take tourists to Fern Grotto.

Although, technically, Fern Grotto as a state park could be visited by anyone with a boat or kayak, in practice it was the private property of the two commercial boat companies and their Native Hawaiian crews.

Mainland *haoles* tying a small boat or kayak to the landing at Fern Grotto were likely to see it untied and drifting down the stream when they returned from touring the cave.

The grotto's decline began with Hurricane Iwa in 1982, accelerated in the 1990s by the collapse of Hawaii's economy and was struck a fatal blow by Hurricane Iniki in 1992.

By 2000, all the Hawaii state parks were in serious disrepair.

The same year, the plantation that operated Reservoir 21 went out of business, the flow of water into the cave stopped and the ferns began to die.

Also in 2000, Waialeale Boat Tours stopped paying rent to the state. In 2004, the state seized the company's boats for back payment.

That left Smith's Boat Services, a subsidiary of Smith's Tropical Paradise (which puts on what is arguably the best luau on Kauai at its tropical botanical gardens at the mouth of the Wailua River) as the sole means of transport of tourists to Fern Grotto.

In most places, that's called a monopoly. But, as tourist attractions go, the dried-up Fern Grotto no longer attracted many tour boat passengers and Smith's trips up the river almost disappeared.

At this juncture, it's probably worth noting that the Smith Family and Mayor Kusaka are tight. Very tight.

Walter "Freckles" Smith II, who inherited the company from his father Walter Smith I, is known as "Kauai's Ambassador of Tourism" and was Kusaka's constant companion on her globe-straddling, taxpayer-funded jaunts to tourist agent conventions.

And, of course, Mayor Bryan Baptiste and Former Mayor Maryanne Kusaka are very tight as well.

So, here was the business of one of Kusaka's dearest friends swirling around the financial drain and here was the HTA ready to spend $250,000 to fix a broken tourist attraction for the sole benefit of the same Smith Family.

And here was Mayor Bryan Baptiste, "Son of Kusaka."

What Baptiste did is unique in the annals of the repair of state parks anywhere in the United States.

And totally illegal, according to state procurement officials.

Baptiste, in effect, said to the State Parks Division: "Rather than fixing Fern Grotto yourself, give me the $250,000 in the form of a grant, I'll toss in $50,000 in in-kind (no actual money) matching and Kauai County will enhance the makeover of Fern Grotto State Park."

State governments rarely—if ever—turn state funds over to a county for construction work on state property. But, with the promise of enhanced value through county matching money, it sounded like too good a deal to pass up.

So, when the Kauai Economic Planning and Development Office sent the state a grant application for the HTA money to repair Fern Grotto, it seemed like a good idea.

Here's where it got illegal:

The Kauai Chamber of Commerce presented a grant proposal to the County of Kauai, offering to run the Fern Grotto Rehab Project.

The grant proposal, prepared by Chamber President Mamo Cummings (now the director of community relations of Princeville Corporation, the largest developer on Kauai's North shore), was word-for-word identical to the grant proposal Kauai County sent the state.

To say this was a done deal from the get-go would be stating the obvious.

The Kauai County Office of Economic Planning and Development took the $250,000 state grant and re-granted it to the Kauai Chamber of Commerce.

The Kauai Chamber of Commerce, without seeking any competitive bids, awarded the contract to Lelan Nishek and Kauai Nursery and Landscaping.

Oh, yeah, and the Chamber was awarded a 10 percent fee—$25,000—for "administering the contract."

Meanwhile, the ever-loyal-to-whatever-mayor-she-works-for Beth Tokioka had been appointed director of the Kauai Office of Economic Planning and Development.

It didn't start out as her project. But, once aboard, that didn't stop her from defending it when a reporter started asking questions about the project.

First, Tokioka said, the Kauai County Council had approved it.

Not exactly.

The meeting minutes (this was one of those rare times the Council met outside of executive session, so the minutes were indisputably public) showed the Council had voted to approve the county accepting the grant from the Hawaii Tourism Authority.

The Kauai Chamber of Commerce was listed among many "participants" in the project in a memo given the Council members.

But no one from Tokioka's office ever told the Council the money would be given to the Chamber so it could award the construction contract without seeking bids or that the Chamber would be paid a $25,000 fee using public funds for administering the project.

Tokioka next insisted both the State Parks Division and the Hawaii Tourism Authority were fully aware of the Chamber's role and approved it.

The State Parks Division head said in an interview with a reporter he knew nothing about the Chamber of Commerce being involved in the project. Ditto the Hawaii Tourism Authority, after a thorough search of their files on the project.

Tokioka next argued that, by law, the Hawaii Tourism Authority was exempt from the state procurement statutes and regulations, so the project was not required to go out for competitive bids.

According to the head of the Hawaii Tourism Authority, only part of what Tokioka said was correct.

The Hawaii Tourism Authority itself legally can award no-bid contracts for goods and services that HTA alone will use.

But what Tokioka neglected to mention was money granted by the Hawaii Tourism Authority to other state and county agencies for public works projects still is covered by state procurement law.

Competitive bidding was absolutely, positively required.

Tokioka next argued that once the money went to a private non-profit organization like the Chamber, the requirement for competitive bids went away because state law doesn't cover a private non-profit agency.

Lloyd Unebasami, chief administrative officer of the Hawaii Tourism Authority and former head of all state purchasing, said he had never heard, in Hawaii or elsewhere, of a private non-profit like the Chamber of Commerce using government money to repair a government facility.

Not only was it illegal without going to bid, it was illegal period, he said.

The chief purchasing officers of all four counties—including Kauai—said exactly the same thing.

Tokioka's next excuse was that since Kauai Nursery was the only company on Kauai capable of Doing the work.

An informal survey of the names painted on the doors of construction vehicles on Kauai's main (and only) highway on any day of any week will show they come from all over Hawaii to do work on Kauai projects. They just throw their gear on a barge and their crews on an airplane, rent some cheap hotel rooms, and go to work.

Maybe in the mayor's mind only Kauai companies should work on Kauai, but that's not what the law says and it's not the reality of construction work in Hawaii.

Tokioka's last card (and it didn't trump anything but give her credit for bleeding her last drop of blood for her mayor) was that, if the Chamber didn't administer the Fern Grotto project, she would have to add a new county employee at taxpayer expense to do it.

But when Tokioka led a press tour of the finished Fern Grotto project in September 2004, Mamo Cummings and the Chamber of Commerce were nowhere in sight. The Chamber wasn't even mentioned.

Asked to provide paperwork showing the Chamber actually had administered the Fern Grotto restoration (and thus earned its $25,000 fee), Tokioka had to admit no such documentation existed.

All she could provide was Mamo Cumming's cut-and-paste grant application copied entirely from a county document, the canceled check from the county to the Chamber, and the sole-source contract with Kauai Nursery.

The project had, in fact, been administered by Tokioka's office after all. No additional county employee had been hired.

The Baptiste shell game appeared again and again through his first term.

He could get County Attorney Lani Nakazawa to opine that whatever he was doing was legal, even if it wasn't.

If you wear the king's uniform, you shoot the king's gun.

Who was going to challenge him? It was the duty of the press, but they lacked the backbone.

It was the duty of the state attorney general, who had been appointed by a Republican governor and the U.S. attorney, who had been appointed by a Republican president.

Republican prosecutors going after a Republican mayor? Not likely.

One more Bryan Baptiste war story serves to illustrate just how twisted this administration was.

The voters of Kauai had been paying skyrocketing property taxes for the past four years because of a sudden real estate boom fueled by mainland speculators.

Baptiste took the usual political step: The mayor appointed a committee to study tax reform. The committee issued a report and recommendations. It is still gathering dust on a shelf.

So a group of activists put their own tax reform solution on the ballot.

In November 2004, the voters, by a 2 to 1 margin, approved a County Charter amendment freezing property values for taxation purposes at 1998 levels.

Baptiste had promised to govern "by the will of the people." Listening to the people was what his endless of Ka Leo town hall meetings were all about.

But when the voters overwhelmingly chose to stop his runaway tax increases (400 percent tax hikes for some property owners), Baptiste did a 180-degree turn.

In a lawsuit likely unique in the history of the United States, Kauai County sued itself, asking the courts to rule the ballot proposition unconstitutional.

Baptiste asked the courts to order the county to ignore the voter-approved change in the Charter.

By naming herself as the plaintiff and Baptiste as the defendant, County Attorney Lani Nakazawa represented both sides in the dispute.

The theory behind the lawsuit was that the state Constitution vests all budget-making authority ("the power of the purse") in the legislative bodies of the state and counties.

That is: Only the County Council can approve a budget, and the voters can't change it (even though they have a right of initiative, referendum and recall in the Kauai County Charter).

But the Constitution does not limit the ability of the people to change tax laws through a Charter amendment. And that was what the voters did.

In "her" lawsuit against the county, Nakazawa argued that the voters, had illegally limited the budget by approving a property valuation rollback. She said that power was reserved exclusively for the County Council.

She asked the court to issue an order prohibiting Baptiste from complying with the Charter amendment.

In most jurisdictions, courts generally rule that the vote of the people trumps most technical or legal flaws in the ballot language. The will of the people was very clear in this vote.

Courts also generally rule that if there are technical or legal flaws in the language of a ballot question, it should be challenged in court *before* the election, not afterward.

Nonetheless, the ever-helpful Judge George Masuoka of the Fifth Circuit Court ruled the ballot item was unconstitutional.

The Hawaii Supreme Court upheld Masuoka.

In 2006, Baptiste was reelected for another four-year term by a two votes. "One more than I needed," Baptiste chuckled afterward.

There is no automatic recount provision that exists in many other states when the margin of victory is so narrow. The Hawaii Supreme Court refused to order a recount because challengers could not give any examples of voting fraud.

A one-vote margin hardly constitutes an overwhelming endorsement of his first four years in office or a popular mandate for the next term.

. . .

CHAPTER 13: KAIPO ASING

For a decade and a half, Kauai County Council member Bill "Kaipo" Asing was the hero of the small band of "good government" activists on Kauai: A reformer and a smiter of mayors.

Asing cast a bright light into the dark corners of Kauai County government.

The old Asing was the picture of a passionate minority leader, of the loyal opposition, of the independent politician with no ties to special interests (he never spent more than $100 on any campaign).

Asing's own probing of county government's shortcomings was the equal of any investigative journalist.

In one instance, his digging—literally—discovered a pipe serving a fire hydrant at a county dump was not the standard high-capacity, high-volume hardware usually associated with fire fighting. Instead, it was the diameter of the water pipes in a residential home.

Someone in county government had installed a cheap substitute and probably pocketed the difference. The loser was the Kauai Fire Department when the dump caught fire.

Typically, though, there was no investigation by the county to follow up on Asing's allegations. There never is. The fingers might all point to the top.

One of the real failings of Kauai County government is its inability to understand the checks and balances built into American democracy.

There is supposed to be friction between the mayor and the council and the courts and the press.

On Kauai there are no checks or balances. Everyone— including the lapdog press—signs on before any votes are taken. The Council passes a bill, the mayor signs it, the reporters sing its praises.

If it is challenged in court (highly unlikely), the judge blesses it.

In his days as the "Conscience of the County Council," Kaipo Asing was the only one willing to say the emperor was naked.

When Maryanne Kusaka was mayor, she was Asing's favorite target during his televised long-winded "chalk talks" on government ineptitude and corruption at the blackboard during Council meetings.

In turn, Kusaka and her department heads did not conceal the special loathing they reserved only for Asing.

But a funny thing happened when the County Council handed Asing the gavel in 2002. The position was vacated when Ron Kouchi left the Council to run for mayor.

In the blink of an eye, Chairman Asing transformed into a petty tyrant, a champion of closed-door deal-making, and a close ally of newly-elected Mayor Bryan Baptiste in

Baptiste's campaign to purge the Kauai Police Department of *haole* influence.

The activists who show up at every Council meetings to rail against county government all, without exception, adored Kaipo Asing.

For many years, Asing had been saying the things they would say if they could get a seat on the Council.

The instant Asing became Council chairman, everything changed.

The rants Asing formerly aimed at mayors and department heads suddenly were pointed at activists and journalists.

The mere holding of power rather than actually using it for anything constructive appeared to be sufficient reward for Asing. Perhaps he felt he earned it for his many years of being the outsider. He guarded it jealously.

In his first year as chairman, the Council did little at its meetings except approve the minutes of the prior meeting.

When asked about the inaction of the Council, Asing pointed at the mayor and said (correctly) that Baptiste hadn't asked for a single bill during that year.

In 2006, Asing was elected to his 12th term on the Council and his third term as Council chairman.

Between January 2003 and July 2005, the first two and a half years of Asing's chairmanship, the Kauai Council conducted more than 140 executive sessions, according to activist Ray Chuan, who keeps score.

That's an average of 58 executive sessions per year.

In the last two years of Ron Kouchi's chairmanship, the Council averaged 20 executive sessions a year.

Asing had almost tripled the number of executive sessions.

The result was a war between Kauai County and the state Office of Information Practices (OIP), the agency charged with interpreting Hawaii's open meetings and public records laws.

Sadly (although it is clear the politicians want it this way), the OIP has no enforcement powers. If it orders a government agency to open a meeting or its file cabinets, there is nothing the OIP can do if the agency refuses.

It is often said that Hawaii has the best open government laws and the worst enforcement of those laws in the United States.

Under state law, the state Attorney General's Office is supposed to file lawsuits when the OIP is ignored.

In practice, Republican Gov. Linda Lingle's appointed Attorney General Mark Bennett refused to do anything to enforce the open meetings and public records laws unless a private citizen has first taken the agency to court and won.

In keeping the Council chamber door and the file cabinets locked, Asing was ably abetted by County Clerk

Peter Nakamura, a career bureaucrat whose main tactic is to ignore legitimate requests for county records as if they never had been made.

Alternatively, Nakamura charges huge sums for "staff" time to retrieve public records.

When the OIP ordered Nakamura to turn over the 140-plus executive session minutes to two private citizens, Nakamura finally did so and billed them $2,886.75 for "staff time" to look up public records.

In most jurisdictions, a reporter or private citizen wanting to look through government files is pointed to the file cabinets and turned loose, often with a sarcastic "Knock yourself out." comment from the chief bureaucrat in charge.

Not on Kauai.

On Jan. 11, 2005, an OIP attorney told the Kauai County Council staff that the Council would be violating the law if it went ahead with closed-door confirmation hearings for a roster of Baptiste appointee to boards and commissions.

An hour later, Asing thumbed his nose at the OIP and went ahead with the secret sessions.

The previous month, Councilwoman (and former Mayor) JoAnn Yukimura asked OIP for an opinion as to whether closed-door confirmation hearings were legal.

In early January, OIP Director Les Kondo said he was informing Yukimura that the hearings had to be public.

On the morning of January 11, OIP attorney Lorna Aratani told Council staff the planned hearings later that day would violate the law.

"I told them the hearings should not be done in executive session," she said in an interview that day. "I told them a written opinion was being drafted and the OIP's conclusion would be the same as the verbal opinion I was giving them.

"If they insisted on something in writing, I could have written 'No Executive Session' on a piece of paper and faxed it to them," she said.

The Council ran 18 Baptiste appointees through the closed confirmation hearings that day.

Nine days later, on Jan. 20, 2005, the County Council met in what became the highly controversial Executive Session 177. (As a means of identifying them, executive sessions were numbered).

ES 177 was all about the Council investigating the KPD.

The OIP later ruled ES 177 was illegal and ordered the county to make the minutes public.

On April 14, 2005, the OIP answered a request for an opinion from Police Commission Chairman Mike Ching, who was one of the subjects of the ES177 meeting.

After reviewing the secret transcript, the OIP noted:

"It appears a significant portion of that meeting involved discussion of whether the Council should in fact be considering ES 177 in an executive meeting and what specific matter the Council was considering in ES 177."

The OIP ruled that debate should have taken place in public *before* the Council voted on going into ES 177.

"The situation raises the question of how the council can vote to discuss a particular issue in executive session when the particular issue has not been identified," the OIP opinion said.

The second question was whether the matters addressed in ES 177 fit into one or more of the eight specific reasons in state law that allow executive sessions.

The OIP opinion states:

"Prior to convening ES 177, the county attorney represented to OIP that the executive session would include discussions related to sensitive ongoing investigations involving the Federal Bureau of Investigation and the State Attorney General.

"It was further represented that these ongoing investigations involved confidential informants and undercover officers.

"It was asserted that discussions regarding these investigations in a public forum would jeopardize the investigations.

"Based upon the representations made by the county attorney, OIP indicated that it did not appear to be inappropriate for the Council to convene an executive meeting."

Well, guess what? The county attorney lied. There were no "ongoing investigations" discussed.

The OIP opinion goes on to say:

"Upon reviewing the ES 177 minutes there is no indication that the Council considered or discussed any such investigations described by the county attorney."

The OIP said the minutes show the Council discussed three investigations:

- An investigation being conducted by the County of Kauai Ethics Board.

- A KPD investigation that had been turned over to the Kauai county prosecutor.

- A proposed investigation into the termination of a KPD recruit.

The exception to the public meeting law that the county attorney claimed allowed the Council to go into executive session involves "sensitive matters related to public safety or security."

The OIP concluded:

"It is OIP's opinion that the actual matters discussed by the Council in ES 177 fall short of constituting 'related to public safety and security.' Therefore, it is OIP's opinion that the matters discussed and decided on therein should have been done so in a public meeting."

The Kauai County attorney claimed the executive session also was legal under a provision in the law that allows a board to go into closed-door meetings "to consult with its attorney on questions and issues pertaining to the board's powers, duties, privileges, immunities and liabilities."

The Kauai County attorney uses this boilerplate for every executive session conducted by every Kauai County board or commission.

In the sole instance where executive session minutes for a closed County Council meeting "to consult with the board's attorney" were obtained (through the lawsuit filed by the author of this book), the vast majority of the discussion had nothing to do with consulting with the board's attorney.

It's very likely (there's no way to know for sure with minutes that remain eternally sealed) that "consulting with the board's attorney" is simply a Kauai County attorney smokescreen to hide many, many illegally closed meetings on Kauai.

From the OIP opinion on ES 177, that certainly was true in this closed meeting:

"In reviewing the ES 177 minutes, it is OIP's opinion that only an extremely limited portion of the discussion that occurred during ES 177 can reasonably fall within the attorney-client privilege.

"It is our strong recommendation that the Council act to immediately remedy its violation of the Sunshine Law (the public meetings statute) by making public the ES 177 minutes, subject only to the redaction of those limited portions which constitute attorney-client privilege communications."

At Asing's (and County Attorney Lani Nakazawa's) urging, the Kauai County then sued the OIP in an effort to keep the transcript sealed.

Here was an amazing (everywhere except on Kauai) situation: A county government was suing the state to keep public documents from the public.

Even more amazing (but not surprising), the court on Kauai sided with the County. It ruled that items involving attorney-client privilege between the Council and the county attorney were so intermingled with the non-privileged parts of the transcript that it was impossible to determine what was public and what wasn't.

The OIP appealed to the State Intermediate Court of Appeals where a decision still is pending. Even if the OIP eventually wins, the transcripts will be several years old and of little news value. But that's what the Kauai County attorney was hoping for when she sued the OIP.

There are many, many government attorneys outside of Kauai County who would stand up in those instances and say to their client: "No! You can't do that! It's wrong!"

Neither Kauai County Attorney Lani Nakazawa nor any of her staff attorneys appeared to have had that brand of moral fiber. They believed it was their jobs to make the county's illegal acts look legal, even if they knew the law had been violated.

. . .

Part I: Jackie Tokashiki versus KPD

On May 14, 2002, Jackie Tokashiki filed lawsuits in both state and federal court against Freitas and Kauai County.

Beyond the dispute in the lawsuit, Tokashiki's case demonstrates (again) the absurdity of many parts of the hopelessly muddled Kauai County Charter.

Since 1980, Tokashiki had been the private secretary to the police chief (actually a parade of police chiefs) including Freitas. Tokashiki was an "at will" employee, meaning she had no civil service protection and could be fired at the chief's whim.

Under the County Charter, the secretary to the police chief also is the secretary to the Police Ccommission.

The concepts of "conflict of interest" and "separation of powers" apparently never entered the head of the long-ago and long-departed county attorney who first drafted the Kauai County Charter.

Working for both the police chief and the commission that sets policy for the police department was not a conflict Jackie Tokashiki spent any time fretting about for her first 21 years on the job.

But one day in July 2001, Lt. Alvin Seto and Inspector Mel Morris showed up on her doorstep with their laundry list of complaints about Chief Freitas.

According to court records, Tokashiki took off her chief's secretary hat, put on her Police Commission's secretary hat and processed the complaint, sending copies to the members of the commission (including Mayor Kusaka, an ex officio member) and the county attorney.

And she scheduled a special (and obviously closed-door) Commission meeting for Aug. 10, 2001.

She did not send a courtesy copy to the chief.

The reason for the executive session was not posted, a violation, again, of the state Open Meeting Law.

At the same time, still typing away in the chief's office, she prepared a memo for the commissioners outlining the procedure for handling complaints, sent an invitation to Kusaka to attend the meeting (as if she would skip it...) and researched the issue of leave (really suspension) both with and without pay.

She also drafted a letter requesting, apparently by name, John Ko, one of the three investigators for the Honolulu Police Commission, be loaned to Kauai County.

On Aug. 10, the Commission suspended Freitas, although he didn't learn of it until Aug. 13. The written directive Kusaka gave him, drafted by Tokashiki, required Freitas to turn in his gun, badge, identification, pager, cell phone, vehicle and office keys.

When Freitas went to his office a week later, his gun, which he had left in his desk when he was suspended, was gone.

Tokashiki had locked it in a safe, but she lied to Freitas and said she didn't know where it was.

In fact, She had searched Freitas's desk looking for evidence against the chief without any warrant or any authority at all.

Freitas requested the Commission bar Tokashiki from future Commission meetings regarding the investigation of him, and the county attorney told her to stay away.

Ko showed up to conduct the investigation, was given the keys to the chief's car for his use and unpacked at the Kauai Marriott Beach Resort where he would spend the next two months with the county paying all of his expenses.

Ko asked for members of the department to step forward and talk to him about Freitas. Unlike Honolulu, where Ko usually worked, "stepping forward" is not something any local does on Kauai.

Tokashiki was then enlisted to "encourage" members of the department to be interviewed by Ko. She also gave a statement to Ko and was a key witness in the case.

As already noted, the ultimate result of all this sound and fury was two letters of reprimand in the chief's personnel folder: One for giving his fiancé a ride in his police car and the other for yelling at Inspector Mel Morris in a private meeting.

On Jan. 7, 2002, Freitas returned to work as police chief and immediately reassigned Tokashiki to a position as secretary in the Administrative and Technical Services Bureau. Her pay and benefits were unaffected.

On April 26, 2002, Freitas told Tokashiki she was terminated effective May 31.

Two weeks later Tokashiki filed lawsuits in state and federal courts claiming that, even though she was an "at will" employee and could be fired by Freitas at any time, the chief's retaliatory firing of her had violated her job protections under the Hawaii Whistleblower's Protection Act.

In February 2004, Tokashiki's attorney Clayton Ikei (a Honolulu lawyer who for decades has sued Kauai County on behalf of many employees in many departments and come away with many large settlements from the county) took the depositions of the key figures in the case.

Although the facts discovered in the deposition would not become public for another two years, Ikei obtained the first up close look at what was going on at all those closed-door Police Commission sessions.

What the "secret" Police Commission transcripts revealed was that after Nelson Gabriel was acquitted of molesting his stepdaughter, it had become quite clear that Freitas had been on solid legal ground when he refused to allow Lt. Alvin Seto to attempt to coerce Gabriel's wife into lying on the stand.

Here's what happened next that the public never was told:

Commission Chairwoman Dede Wilhelm testified in her deposition that the Commission appeared ready to consider the charge against Freitas of "hindering the prosecution" of Gabriel.

But County Attorney Hartwell Blake slammed on the brakes.

Masuoka issued his ruling in the case against Nelson Gabriel. He found Gabriel innocent.

As a direct result of Masuoka's decision, Blake told the Commission to "lay low on this and cool it" because he had become convinced the charge by Seto and Morris was unfounded.

If the Commission voted to dismiss Freitas for "hindering prosecution," and Freitas sued the Commission, Blake told them his office would not represent them and the county would not pay any damages awarded Freitas.

That little gem had been hidden in the Police Commission's secret executive session minutes for five years until it was revealed by the Hawaii Supreme Court in 2006.

Circuit Judge Masuoka, to no one's amazement, ruled in favor of the county and dismissed Tokashiki's lawsuit. Masuoka ruled her actions were not protected by the Whistleblower's Protection Act.

But her lawyer appealed Masuoka's decision, and on April 11, 2006, the Hawaii Supreme Court overturned Masuoka and ordered the case be set for trial.

As usual, the trial never took place. Kauai County was willing to pay a lot of taxpayer dollars to keep its dirty laundry from public view.

More than a year later, in May 2007, Kauai County settled the lawsuit and paid Tokashiki $325,000.

Once again, the settlement was approved by the County Council in an executive session that should have been conducted in public. The topic was not noted on the Council agenda for the meeting.

And the county made no announcement of the settlement. It was leaked to the local newspaper on Kauai.

• • •

CHAPTER 15: A STAMPEDE TO THE COURTHOUSE

Part II: Mark Begley versus KPD

On April 8, 2003, KPD Officer Mark Begley filed a lawsuit against his employers in federal court in Honolulu.

Mark Begley found the fastest (and most bizarre) track to promotion in the history of the KPD. In 2003, Begley, then a patrolman, sued the department claiming he was beaten and suffered permanent brain damage when he tried to expose an organized crime ring within the KPD. His lawsuit was tossed out by a federal judge. Three and a half years later, Begley was named deputy chief of the Kauai Police Department.

Begley's lawsuit was prepared using the legal strategy of "throw lots of mud at the wall and see what sticks."

Some of it may well have been true but there is so much overkill in the allegations that it was impossible to figure out which parts to believe.

It is educational to note that Begley's attorney, Mark Zenger, later filed a similar scattergun lawsuit against the Kauai Fire Department on behalf of a Kauai lifeguard charging the KFD brass with everything but the attack on Pearl Harbor.

Begley's lawsuit alleges:

- That Lt. Martin Curnan, at the time the head of the Vice Squad (which also, more importantly, is the de-facto Narcotics Squad on an island where marijuana is a major cash crop) was a member of a criminal organization that included both KPD officers and civilians. The organization allegedly was in the business of officers seizing drugs from drug dealers but not turning the drugs in as evidence.

- That a KPD officer twice went to Kapaa High School and took possession of narcotics seized from students by school administrators. Allegedly, no police reports ever were filed by the officer and the drugs never were turned in as evidence.

- That when Begley complained to Chief Freitas, his complaint was ignored.

- That Curnan allegedly assaulted Begley, hitting him on the head so hard that he had to be flown by air ambulance to an Oahu hospital where he was treated for brain damage that has left him permanently disabled.

- That a woman who worked as a KPD confidential informant alleged that drugs she obtained in "controlled buys" were kept by Curnan and arrests never were made.

- That she also claimed she told the Curnan about two drug-related murders that never were investigated.

- That the same woman claimed she was raped by a relative of Curnan's and was told the rape was a warning to keep her mouth shut about Curnan's activities.

- That all of the members of the Vice Squad were either members of the criminal organization or had promised Curnan to ignore it.

Curnan retired. The case droned on for four years and finally came to trial before a federal magistrate (there was no jury). The magistrate ruled for Kauai County.

The only allegation that could be shown to be true is that Begley was in a fight and received permanent brain damage that has left him with a sometimes headache and a constant ringing in his left ear.

It was true Begley had been drinking at an abandoned sugar mill with Curnan and a civilian friend of Curnan's named David Nawai.

Begley testified it was not uncommon for Vice Squad members to meet at remote locations for the purpose of getting very drunk both on and off duty, sort of the Kauai variant of Joseph Wambaugh's novel, *The Choir Boys*.

Begley admitted he was so drunk he couldn't recall who hit him.

Curnan and Nawai claimed Begley took a swing at Nawai and Nawai hit him in self-defense. They said Begley's head hit the pavement and, when they carried Begley to his truck to drive him home, Begley's head accidentally hit the door frame.

The filing of Begley's lawsuit reignited efforts in the mayor's office to oust Freitas. It appeared clear Baptiste had been given a mandate to "Get Freitas" by his mentor, Maryanne Kusaka.

"We have a duty to seek the truth for our citizens," pronounced new Mayor Bryan Baptiste, commenting on Begley's charges.

During his tenure on the County Council, Baptiste never met an executive session or a locked government file cabinet that he did not love. "Seeking the truth" wasn't exactly one of his virtues.

Baptiste announced he would call in the FBI.

Obviously, the county had learned from the Seto fiasco that all the Kauai Police Commission knew how to do was spend huge amounts of money to prove nothing.

The FBI wouldn't cost Kauai County a cent and Baptiste liked anything he could get for free from the state or the feds.

Freitas said he had investigated every one of Begley's claims and found nothing to turn over to the county prosecutor.

The chief said he would welcome an FBI probe and publicly urged his officers to cooperate.

Whether or not the FBI ever looked into Begley's allegations will never be known. But no charges ever were filed by federal prosecutors. It can be assumed they found no basis for Begley's accusations.

It would be easy to assume that Begley would never return to work at a department he considered so evil and corrupt.

That would be a false assumption.

Limited to a desk job by his "permanent brain damage," Begley's star immediately began to rise.

In fact his fast-track promotions up the KPD chain of command were nothing less than meteoric.

He became the KPD's recruiting officer, quite literally the department's poster child.

Begley was named "Police Officer of the Year" by the Kauai Police Commission.

In August 2007, Begley was promoted to lieutenant.

In November 2007, with less than three months in grade as a lieutenant, Begley was chosen by newly appointed Chief Darryl Perry as his deputy chief.

Asked how a chronic malcontent who had made outrageous charges against the KPD, none of which ever were proven, became deputy chief, former Chief K.C. Lum shrugged his shoulders: "That's politics on Kauai."

· · ·

CHAPTER 16: A STAMPEDE TO THE COURTHOUSE

Part III: Alvin Seto versus KPD

Former KPD Lt. Alvin Seto, who had moved on to become a security supervisor at the Navy's Pacific Missile range, filed his own lawsuit against Freitas and Kauai County one month after Begley's.

Seto, a 22-year KPD veteran, had quit the force in May, 2002. He filed his lawsuit on May 27, 2003, just under the wire to meet the one-year statute of limitations deadline.

Seto's attorney was Clayton Ikei, the same lawyer representing Jackie Tokashiki in her lawsuit against Freitas and the county.

And the case was filed in federal court in Honolulu.

As an investigating officer, Seto won many criminal cases in Judge George Masuoka's court. But when it came to a civil case against Kauai County, Seto was well aware of Masuoka's track record of favoring the county. So, he went to U.S. District Court.

The basis of the lawsuit was the same accusation Seto made against Freitas two years earlier: That Freitas had "hindered" the prosecution of Nelson Gabriel on 22 charges of sexually molesting his step-daughter.

When he heard about Seto's lawsuit, Freitas was furious.

"I'm done with saying 'no comment.' How many times does he get to make this same complaint and how many times do we have to prove there isn't any truth to it?" he asked.

What Seto alleged Freitas had done was to prohibit Seto from illegally using a sexual harassment complaint against Nelson that Seto had coerced out of a police dispatcher.

Seto planned to use that information in an attempt to strong-arm Gabriel's wife into testifying against her husband. Mrs. Gabriel was prepared to tell the court her daughter had a long record of lying when people made her angry, including falsely charging them with sexually abusing her.

Freitas said the county attorney advised him any mention of a pending sexual harassment charge would be a violation of federal law and Seto could not reveal it to Gabriel's wife.

Seto had tried to convince County Prosecutor Michael Soong to charge Freitas with "hindering prosecution," but Soong said there was no case and he refused to file charges.

Seto then went to Mayor Maryanne Kusaka and the Kauai Police Commission. After many months of investigation and closed-door meetings, Freitas was absolved of "hindering prosecution" by the Police Commission on the advice of the county attorney.

The police dispatcher already had sued Seto and Kauai County for violating her right to anonymity when she reluctantly filed the sexual harassment charge against Nelson. The county settled that case for $100,000.

Yet here was Seto in federal court with exactly the same allegation no one else would believe.

In November 2005, in another of its illegal closed-door sessions, the Kauai County Council agreed to pay Seto $120,000 to settle the case.

Seto received more than the dispatcher he had wronged.

Kauai County never announced the settlement, even though every expenditure of taxpayer money is supposed to be public record. Once again, a newspaper reporter found out about it—six months after it was done.

No reason was given for paying off Seto. Clearly, no one on the Council wanted to brag about it.

• • •

CHAPTER 17: FORMER POLICE CHIEF GEORGE FREITAS

On Oct. 21, 2003, George Freitas announced he would retire as chief of police effective Oct. 31.

Freitas stopped short of saying he was being forced out by Mayor Bryan Baptiste.

But, obviously, he was.

"Was I contacted about retiring or did I initiate the contact?" Freitas asked. "I was contacted."

Freitas was "asked to retire" on the day he returned from his honeymoon.

Exactly what options were open to Freitas other than to accept the buyout never have been made clear.

It was obvious the county attorney had worn down yet another opponent. Freitas was not willing to pay the lawyer fees to keep fighting.

Forced retirement wasn't all gloom for Freitas, who had just turned 60. The county paid him $200,000 in compensation (again approved in a Council secret meeting) for taking early retirement rather than finishing out his contract with the county.

He already was receiving a pension from the Richmond (Calif.) Police Department where he had been an assistant chief.

His new bride, Elizabeth, was a retired Richmond police detective with her own pension and already had established a business administering polygraph tests and working as a private investigator for several private attorneys on Kauai.

Although his name is on the door with Elizabeth's in the family investigations firm, from all appearances Elizabeth does most of the detecting while George prowls the island's many golf courses.

If the mayor and Council publicly thanked Freitas for his many years of service, wished him well and gave him a gold watch, it must have happened in an executive session.

With Freitas out of the picture, Mayor Baptiste could now "fix" the broken KPD.

• • •

CHAPTER 18: THE SHORT REIGN OF ACTING CHIEF WILLIE IHU

Willie Ihu, who had served as acting chief while Freitas was suspended, also was named acting chief when Freitas retired.

Like every other key KPD figure in this tale, Ihu also is tied to the Lap Dancing Incident.

According to his own testimony in the trail of Randy Machado, Ihu was told by Machado what was going on. He never investigated, never filed a complaint against the officers and never was disciplined for failing to do so.

Ihu served only seven months as acting chief. He then retired on May 1, 2004, and was replaced by Acting Chief K.C. Lum.

Ihu was around just long enough to demonstrate how acceptable racism is within KPD.

In 2004, a dog belonging to a local farmer attacked and killed a 17-month-old white boy on Kauai's north shore.

According to several sources who said they heard the police radio conversation, the dispatcher told a KPD supervisor to proceed to the scene immediately. The supervisor reportedly replied, "No hurry, it's just a *haole* kid."

Truston Heart Liddle was the 17-month-old blond-haired toddler killed by a chained dog owned by a local farmer. There was no fence around the dog.

The dog was destroyed but no charges—such as negligent homicide or reckless endangerment, for example—were ever filed against its owner. Its owner was local. Truston was white.

Truston was the grandson of Greg Liddle of Kapaa, one of Hawaii's most famous surfboard "shapers" or designers.

On Feb. 24, 2004, Truston was with his parents—Damon "Dove" Liddle and his wife Raven—on a small farm where they grew organic vegetables. While his parents were working, the child wandered onto an adjoining farm where several dogs were chained or caged.

Truston walked up to a 40-pound un-neutered male dog, which attacked him.

According to Dr. Becky Rhodes, director of the Kauai Humane Society, chaining a dog guarantees the animal will turn mean. "The dog will attack anyone or anything that comes within the radius of its chain," she said.

Truston's six-year-old brother saw the attack and ran to his parents. They found the dog still biting Truston as he lay on the ground.

The couple put the injured child in their car and headed for a medical clinic in Kilauea, calling for help on their cell phone. The police dispatcher told them to stop along the road and wait for firefighters, an ambulance, and police who already were on their way.

Truston was taken to Wilcox Memorial Hospital where he died in the emergency room of multiple head, neck, and chest wounds.

Acting Police Chief Ihu decided because Truston had wandered onto the neighbor's unfenced property because his parents were not supervising him, there was no crime on the part of the local farmer who owned the dog.

The officer who made the "just a *haole* kid" remark over the police radio never has been identified officially.

According to the KPD, the tape of the radio conversation was "accidentally erased."

But according to numerous sources, when he heard about the "just a *haole* kid" transmission, Acting Chief Ihu literally ran to the dispatcher's office and immediately confiscated, bagged and tagged the tape as "evidence" to keep it from becoming public, even though he decided there were no criminal charges to pursue.

. . .

CHAPTER 19: A STAMPEDE TO THE COURTHOUSE

Part IV: Darla Abbatiello versus KPD

On Sept. 8, 2004, Officer Darla Abbatiello filed a lawsuit in federal court in Honolulu claiming her civil rights and her protection under the Whistleblowers' Protection Act were violated when she was punished for reporting a KPD sergeant whom she turned in for selling protection to a drug dealer.

Abbatiello carries with her a ton of credibility. In 1999, she was named "Police Officer of the Year" for all of Hawaii.

She also is one of the best-liked police officers on Kauai.

In the old Kauai County Courthouse people scheduled to appear in court (including KPD officers) used to wait in a huge foyer lined with wooden chairs. It was not unusual to see Abbatiello carrying around one or more babies.

Routinely, she would go up to mothers with children, who had been trapped in the waiting area for hours, and offer to watch their children while they went outside for a smoke. Her kindness paid off in lots of tips over the years.

And, like so many others in this tale, Abbatiello had a tie to the Lap Dancing Incident in 1995. According to testimony at Officer Randy Machado's criminal trial, Machado's comments to Abbatiello were so sexist and disgusting, one of the prostitutes told him to knock it off.

She was on duty in Waimea and was brought in to search the women dancers arrested that night.

Abbatiello was one of only five women officers on the KPD and the first ever to be assigned to the Vice Squad. Given the troubled history of the Vice Squad, her assignment was a highly mixed blessing.

In her lawsuit, Abbatiello said that in December 2003 she obtained a warrant to search the home of the girlfriend of a major drug supplier who had been arrested the previous June with two pounds of crystal methamphetamine in his possession.

According to the lawsuit, Sgt. Irvil Kapua, who was not a member of the vice unit, went to Abbatiello's commanding officer and told him Abbatiello should not be investigating the case.

Vice warrants are confidential and Kapua should not have known about the investigation, the lawsuit contends.

The lawsuit also alleges that Kapua registered the suspect as a confidential informant in violation of department policy.

When Abbatiello told Kapua her real target was the woman's boyfriend who had been arrested in June, Kapua allegedly told Abbatiello the man was "nothing" and "small time."

The woman suspect did no work as an informant and on Dec. 26, Abbatiello arrested her.

After the arrest, the woman told Abbatiello that her boyfriend had paid Kapua $6,000 to protect both of them, according to the lawsuit.

Abbatiello reported the suspect's statement to her supervisor and an investigation was opened but allegedly never pursued.

As of the filing of her lawsuit almost a year later, "no meaningful action has been taken in either the criminal or internal investigations," her lawsuit stated.

After Abbatiello filed her complaint against Kapua, he repeatedly threatened her both in the police station and in public places, her lawsuit contends.

Abbatiello requested a temporary transfer to the patrol division to avoid Kapua.

Instead, she was given a permanent transfer to patrol duty and her salary was cut by two pay grades, neither of which she had requested.

Shortly afterward, Abbatiello opened her desk dictionary to find arrows pointing to the word "death" and her name written in ink beside it. She claimed the threat never had been investigated.

Instead, her lawsuit claims, she was ordered to use the back door to the police department and to stay away from Kapua.

In an amended complaint filed the following year, Abbatiello claimed she was retaliated against again when she refused an order that she believed would violate the civil rights of two women suspects.

The women both were arrested at Lihue Airport. Abbatiello was ordered to conduct strip searches of the two women, which she did, even though she questioned the warrant, which did not specifically authorize strip searches.

She then was ordered to photograph all the body cavities of the two women. At that point, she refused because of the lack of authority in the warrant.

The department allegedly retaliated by rescinding her status as a field training officer for which she received extra pay for breaking in rookie patrolmen. They also refused to give her any overtime assignments even though every officer on the KPD was working overtime.

The case was set for trial in December 2007.

A month before the trial date, the Kauai County Council agreed to settle the lawsuit by paying Abbatiello $1 million, by far a record in KPD cases.

Sgt. Kapua, who was accused of threatening to kill Abbatiello and who called her a "fucking cunt" numerous times in front of numerous witnesses, never was disciplined and never was charged with any crimes for allegedly taking protection money from a drug dealer.

He retired shortly after the lawsuit was settled.

• • •

CHAPTER 20: HOP SING

K.C. Lum, then 55, a 22-year KPD veteran, was named acting chief of police in May 2004 to replace Willie Ihu, who retired as acting chief.

As with so many of the KPD officers in this story, Lum is tied to the Lap Dancing Incident.

He was a lieutenant at the time and the senior officer on the team that pulled off the sting operation on Fanta-See.

Although it was several weeks after the incident, Lum was the first KPD officer to conduct an extensive interview of Monica Alves on her allegations against Randy Machado and the other officers who took her into the watch sergeant's office.

His report became the basis of the charges against the five KPD officers who molested Alves.

Lum was one of only two KPD officers of Chinese descent. He was raised as a US Army brat on a series of military posts. He was not a Kauai native but he spent his entire police career on the KPD.

Despite his service on the police department, he was an outsider.

When Acting Chief Willie Ihu retired Lum was selected as acting chief and was chosen by the Police Commission to be the next permanent chief.

His swearing-in ceremony at the new KPD headquarters was a strange affair.

It was packed with young patrolmen.

But there were few sergeants, no lieutenants and no assistant chiefs.

He was being shunned by the local "old guard" in a very public way.

Kauai Police Chief K.C. Lum (left)on the day he filed a civil rights lawsuit against Kauai County. Leon Gonsalves, Mayor Bryan Baptiste's only appointee on the Kauai Police Commission when Lum was hired, called the new chief "Hop Sing," a racial slur to Chinese-Americans, the day before Lum was sworn in. The Chinese-American community on Kauai was furious. With Lum when he filed his lawsuit were Dr. Raymond Chuan (center) and former Police Commission Chairman Stanton Pa, both Chinese-American.

The other two finalists for the chief's job were Lt. Regina Ventura, the senior female officer on the KPD and then head of the Vice Squad (which seems to be at the center of every legal controversy), and Maj. Darryl Perry, a retired member of the Honolulu Police Department but a Kauai native.

Perry was the candidate of the KPD old guard.

Lum never was accused of any misconduct in office. Try as they might, Baptiste and the County Council could find nothing to use against him at the Police Commission.

But he was forced—by Mayor Baptiste and the County Council (*not* the Police Commission, the only entity with the legal authority to fire a police chief on Kauai)—to retire on June 7, 2006, with more than three years remaining on his contract.

There are lots of players in this theater of the absurd.

But the leader of the band in the effort to oust Lum clearly was County Councilman Mel Rapozo.

A decade prior, he was Sgt. Mel Rapozo, the KPD supervisor who stood off to the side and smirked while four KPD patrolmen fondled Monica Alves in Rapozo's office. He did nothing to stop them.

The math is simple: Rapozo was a bad cop who took a fall, ended up on the County Council, saw his opportunity to punish Lum, who had reported him for his role in the Alves incident, and seized it.

The other key player was Leon Gonsalves, a retired cop who was the only member of the Police Commission appointed by Baptiste and the only police commissioner to vote against Lum. Gonsalves was a longtime friend of Perry's.

More important, Gonsalves was the one whose blatant racist comment about Lum lit the fuse on everything else that happened.

On Oct. 14, 2004, the day before Lum was sworn in as chief and Ron Venneman (a retired LAPD detective who was one of the very few white members of the KPD) became deputy chief, Gonsalves sent an email to a friend at the Kauai County Prosecutor's Office.

There was no question he was upset that two *haoles*, two "outsiders," were going to be the top two officials of the KPD.

"Tomorrow is the swearing in for Hop Sing and Little Joe, I wouldn't be there, thank Good (sic). I might throw up," Gonsalves wrote.

The email was forwarded many times all over Kauai.

Both Hop Sing and Little Joe were characters on the long-running television pre-political-correctness western *Bonanza*.

Hop Sing was the cook for the Cartwright family, the central characters in the series, and intended solely as a comic figure. He was easily excited and often defended his kitchen with a meat cleaver.

Hop Sing wore a skull cap and a long pigtail. Chinese-Americans saw him as a negative cultural stereotype and being called "Hop Sing" was definitely not a compliment.

K.C. Lum is Chinese-American. So is Mike Ching, at that time the chairman of the Kauai Police Commission. Another member of the Police Commission, Stanton Pa, although his name is Hawaiian, also is part Chinese.

Even Kauai's most strident political activist, Ray Chuan, who has a PhD in physics, is Chinese (although, because he's lived most of his life on the mainland, Chuan is considered a *haole* by locals).

Little Joe was the youngest of the Cartwright sons. He was played by actor Michael Landon (real name Eugene Orowitz), who was Jewish. Ron Venneman, the new deputy chief, is Jewish.

Gonsalves insisted he had called Lum Hop Sing for many years without any complaints he was being racist.

He said he nicknamed Venneman Little Joe because the television character had long curly hair of which he was quite proud and Venneman similarly placed a lot of emphasis on how he combed his hair.

"It's not about prejudice," Gonsalves said shortly afterward. "I don't like it. It's just turned into something that was not supposed to be," said Gonsalves, who is Hawaiian and Portuguese, in an interview shortly afterward.

"I have daughters-in-law who are *haole*, Japanese, Filipino. My grandchildren are all mixed up like chop suey, and I love every one of them," he said.

He added he didn't even know either Venneman or Landon was Jewish.

"To me, Ron looks like Little Joe. I don't know what religion he is," Gonsalves said, adding what certainly reflects the "they all look like to me" attitude of locals:

"I look at a Caucasian and to me he's a *haole*. I don't distinguish between German or Irish or whatever.

"As long as you don't add any adjectives to the term, *haole* just means he's foreigner. There's nothing wrong with being a *haole*.

"I've already apologized. There isn't anything else I can do."

By mainland political standards it was time for Mayor Bryan Baptiste (who, like Gonsalves, is Hawaiian and Portuguese) to immediately step up and give an angry and impassioned speech about how he won't tolerate racism or racist comments in county government.

Instead, Baptiste fanned the flames by doing nothing. His sole comment on Gonsalves's email was that it was "inappropriate."

The mayor knew that the vast majority of his local constituents used racial slurs in everyday conversation.

And he wanted a second term.

But, in the meanwhile, Gonsalves's comments were getting national media attention.

And Chinese-Americans on Kauai (a very small minority; because most Chinese sugar workers on Kauai migrated to Honolulu when they left the plantations) were getting angry.

Violet Hee, the 85-year-old president of the Chinese Cultural Heritage of Kauai, called for Gonsalves to resign immediately.

Lum was threatening to file a civil rights lawsuit in federal court accusing Gonsalves (who technically was one of his bosses) with racism and creating a hostile work environment.

So, Baptiste had to come up with a plan.

And he did. It actually was more a script on which Gonsalves and the County Council agreed beforehand how to play their roles.

On Nov. 5, 2004, Baptiste announced he had asked Gonsalves to resign from the Kauai Police Commission and Gonsalves refused.

Gonsalves confirmed the mayor's press release: "I talked to the mayor last night and I told him I don't think I'll resign."

Baptiste said in his press release (he wasn't, of course, available for questions) that he would ask the Kauai County Council to remove Gonsalves from office.

The Council had approved Gonsalves's appointment, so now they must disapprove it in order for Gonsalves to be removed, the mayor had decided.

No one could remember a member of a county board or commission being removed. And there was nothing in the County Charter about it.

So, it never was clear whether Baptiste or the County Council should have the final word on firing Gonsalves.

Clearly, Baptiste was scurrying for cover. He didn't want to speak out against racism. So he dumped it on the County Council.

His letter to the Council asking it to fire Gonsalves was hardly a stand against racial discrimination:

"My decision to request Mr. Gonsalves's removal from the (Police) Commission has little to do with whether his remarks in the controversial email message were racially prejudiced or not."

And, knowing their constituents would consider a Council firing of Gonsalves a criticism of their racist local culture, the Council did nothing for six months.

Finally, in April, 2005, the Council voted to deny the mayor's request to remove Gonsalves. Gonsalves continued to serve as on the Police Commission.

On Feb. 7, 2006, Lum filed a $1.2 million federal civil rights suit against Kauai County alleging he was the target of discrimination and retaliation because he is an American of Chinese descent.

Lum said the conspiracy between the mayor, County Council and numerous unidentified KPD officers was caused by his insistence on change in the KPD and "to enforce the law no matter where the chips may fall."

Lum's attorney is Clayton Ikei, who had represented Jackie Tokashiki and Alvin Seto.

"The facts speak clearly," Ikei said at the press conference announcing Lum's lawsuit.

"Chief Lum and the reforms he undertook were successful, but they were a threat to the entrenched guard in the police department and in the county—those with a vested interest in preserving the status quo."

A federal judge dismissed Gonsalves as a defendant. Lum has appealed that decision to the 9th U.S. Circuit Court of Appeals and the lawsuit against the county is on hold until the 9th Circuit rules.

• • •

CHAPTER 21: THE ETHICS BOARD AND MICHAEL CHING

The Kauai Ethics Board is not the champion of the public interest and scourge of rotten politicians and bureaucrats that its name implies.

Quite the opposite.

The Ethics Board is a cudgel the mayor wields to smite public officials who criticize him. For starters, the board is made up entirely of the mayor's cronies.

Ethics boards, where they exist in jurisdictions on the mainland, have their own staff and their own lawyers and their own office space outside the government complex.

They operate at "arms length" from the government. Their independence is the sole source of their credibility.

The Hawaii State Ethics Board is not beholden to any one politician. It is appointed by a commission whose members are selected by a variety of elected officials who often have competing interests.

But at the county level in Hawaii, ethic board members are appointed solely by the mayor; a system guaranteed to be abused by unethical mayors.

In 2007, the Hawaii Legislature passed a bill requiring the ethics commissions of the four counties to adopt the state's method of choosing ethics commissioners to insure similar independence.

For the counties in general and Kauai in particular, the bill was a major step toward giving their ethics boards a touch of badly needed credibility.

The bill received zero attention in the media. "Government news is boring" is the mantra of editors. Best stick to helicopter crashes, shark bites, and celebrities making fools of themselves.

Bryan Baptiste, who very much wanted to keep the Kauai Ethics Board as his personal hammer for exacting revenge on political enemies, urged Gov. Linda Lingle to veto the bill.

She did. But it appeared headed for an override vote, and the mayor of Kauai again leaped into action.

Baptiste lobbied legislators to *not* override Lingle's veto.

They didn't. The override never even came up for a vote.

Kauai County Ethics Board members remain the mayor's appointed stooges.

On Kauai, the Board of Ethics has neither independence nor credibility. The board exists to give the impression that county government has integrity, but the reality is just the opposite.

On Kauai, the board's staff is a part of and physically located in the mayor's office.

Every complaint to the Board of Ethics comes through the mayor's office and there is no mechanism preventing the mayor or his staff from seeing every one of them before the board does.

Considering the complaints it receives invariably are about the mayor or members of his administration, it might seem wise to put them at least in some other office, if only for appearance's sake.

And the Board of Ethics's legal advice is provided by the county attorney, who is appointed by the mayor to represent him and his department heads, exactly the same people named in the complaints filed by citizens.

Isn't there a conflict of interest somewhere in there?

Not on Kauai.

Consider the Ethics Board and its investigation of Police Commission Chairman Mike Ching.

The Ethics Board case was entitled "in re: Michael Ching" but the real target, and everyone knew it, was K.C. Lum, who never was the subject of any ethics complaint.

In fact, Lum never was accused anywhere by anyone of doing anything illegal or unethical. His only crime was in being an outsider.

So Baptiste had to figure out a way to back door his effort to get rid of Lum.

Baptiste turned to County Attorney Lani Nakazawa.

Throughout her tenure as Kauai County attorney, Nakazawa was very careful to give all her opinions to county officials verbally, rather than in writing, which would leave a paper trail (assuming, in the first place, anyone ever obtains access to the records, which she made sure was impossible without a long and expensive court fight).

According to county records, the Ethics Board complaint against Ching was filed by Lt. Scott Yagihara, who filed a similar complaint against Police Commission Vice-Chairwoman Carol Furtado.

Yagihara, in fact, soon was littering the County Building with complaints. It became clear he was nothing but an errand boy for Bryan Baptiste.

Furtado called it "another witch hunt" by the mayor and Council.

Mike Ching, a very successful Hanalei businessman who owns and runs a shopping center founded by his father, was the chairman of the Kauai Police Commission when it chose K.C. Lum both as acting chief and later as permanent chief.

It became fairly clear that somewhere in the year-long process to find a replacement for George Freitas, Ching began to favor Lum as the best candidate.

There is nothing in the law to prevent a member of any commission from taking a position on an issue and trying to convince fellow commissioners to do the same.

But there is a Kauai County Ethics Rule forbidding a county official from using their government position to benefit themselves or their friends.

The ethical prohibition was aimed at instances such as Mayor Maryanne Kusaka quadrupling her own travel budget so she could lease a car from her campaign manager. Or, Kusaka using her county-financed television show to promote her best friend's new subdivision.

The Ethics Board thought that was just fine.

But what if a member of a county commission tries to convince fellow commissioners to vote a certain way?

That's why commissions have multiple members and have meetings to debate issues and try to sway fellow members.

Unless, in doing so, you piss off the mayor.

Then the Ethics Board responded to a complaint from a KPD officer (Lt. Yagihara) who never had any personal involvement in the issue or personal knowledge of the allegations he made.

In fact, Yagihara never was called as a witness (odd, because he was in theory the complainant and supposedly a victim of the unethical behavior) at the Ethics Board hearing on the allegations against Ching.

Ching's case went to a hearing officer, E. John McConnell, a retired judge from Maui. He conducted a hearing on Nov. 18, 2005.

On Feb. 23, 2006, McConnell issued his "Findings of Fact and Conclusions of Law" and a separate and much shorter Hearing Officer's Report.

In the end, McConnell found Ching had violated the county's Ethics Code but had NOT broken any laws or violated the County Charter.

Specifically, he found Ching used his position to benefit Lum by supporting Lum's candidacy.

But the retired judge added an important caveat that later would be ignored by Baptiste and the County Council.

McConnell noted in his finding that many people would regard Ching promoting Lum for police chief as a normal part of the political process and his finding could be appealed.

When a judge says that, he is asking to have the issue appealed in court because he really isn't certain himself.

Ching never appealed. Again, it was a question of a private individual with limited resources going against Kauai County with unending resources and a clear willingness to spend as much public money as they needed to win in a courtroom.

McConnell also found that Ching had improperly lobbied the head of the police union on Kauai, Officer Bryson Ponce, to support Lum for chief.

To this day, Ching insists it was the other way around and that Ponce lobbied him.

Ching agrees the two did chat at a table outside a restaurant in Ching's shopping center. But he says he absolutely did not solicit the union's support.

But what's really important is this:

McConnell's findings in the Ching case in no way conclude that Lum was illegally appointed police chief because Ching, although he marginally violated an ethics rule, in no way broke the law.

But that was enough for Baptiste to get rid of Lum, and he did so in a very strange manner.

. . .

CHAPTER 22: TAIL GUNNER MEL

Even while the Ethics Board was stamping out evil on the Police Commission in late 2005, the Kauai County Council was ramping up for an all-out attack on Lum.

The leader, of course, was Councilman Mel Rapozo, the disgraced former KPD sergeant of Lap Dancing fame.

The first volley was a three-hour Council grilling of Lum in September 2005 over the fact his department expenses were running $300,000 over budget.

Even before the meeting, Council members all knew the problem was overtime pay because the KPD was perpetually below strength and officers frequently were called in on their days off to make up the shortfall.

The overtime shortfall wasn't exactly a news flash. The situation had been going on for years before Lum became chief, due in great part to the refusal of two mayors to seek recruits from the mainland.

The Council members also knew that every other county department but one had run over budget the previous fiscal year.

It wasn't much of a charge but it was the only thing they could even attempt to hang around Lum's neck.

And it was a quick and easy way for the Council to kick off its witch hunt.

"I believe the overtime issue is out of control," said Rapozo.

The fact is that a decade after the Lap Dancing Incident, Rapozo maintained very close ties with the middle management of KPD who had fought reform by Freitas and were fighting reform by Lum.

In Council meetings, Rapozo gave the impression (and many in the public believed it) that he wanted to modernize the KPD. In fact, he was working to keep it as provincial and backward as he could.

What happened next was a monumental leap by the County Council into the realm of McCarthyism.

In December 2005, the County Council voted unanimously to invoke its own investigative powers, which exist in the County Charter but never had been used in the history of Kauai County.

The Council gave itself subpoena power, the power to hire additional staff, and the power to conduct secret hearings.

Council members made it clear their targets were Chief Lum and the Police Commission.

Their action was a response to a complaint filed by the mysterious Lt. Scott Yagihara, the same officer who had filed the Ethics Board complaints against Ching and Furtado.

Yagihara has not testified under oath before any public body. He certainly hasn't talked to the press.

On Jan. 31, 2006, Mayor Bryan Baptiste formally asked the Kauai Police Commission to fire Lum.

Baptiste's reasons were lame:

"I have made numerous requests of Chief Lum to improve and increase communications with the Mayor's Office but have seen no evidence of that happening," Baptiste said in his letter to the Police Commission.

At least one of the requests from Baptiste (and Nakazawa) came at a meeting with Lum at which the mayor attempted to strong arm the police chief into filing a phony criminal charge to try to intimidate the author of this book.

Lum refused to file a bogus charge. So Baptiste asked the Police Commission to fire Lum.

Again, the impossibly vague wording of the County Charter doesn't define "cause" for removing a police chief.

Baptiste's call for firing Lum came less than a week after the police union had announced it had worked out its disagreements with Lum and was withdrawing its call for his removal.

"There was hope for the community to move this forward and right after that we get this letter from the mayor," said Carole Furtado, who had become chairwoman of the Police Commission.

Furtado said that what the Police Commission needed to investigate were "the factions within the department," a subject that repeatedly was swept under the rug.

Racism in the KPD remained a topic that no one on Kauai wanted to discuss, let alone investigate.

"We have had this issue, to my knowledge, for the last three or four chiefs, and it has not gotten any better," Furtado said.

On Feb. 6, 2006, Lum filed his discrimination lawsuit in federal court.

Ten days later, responding to the request from Mayor Bryan Baptiste, the Kauai Police Commission voted to initiate a lengthy process to conduct its own investigation of Lum.

This was in addition to the investigative powers the County Council already had given itself.

In late March, Michael Ching resigned from the Police Commission.

Rapozo insisted, "There is no concerted effort by this Council to get rid of Ching or Lum."

But his remarks rang hollow after he repeatedly had said Lum was not qualified and should not have been appointed chief.

Then, suddenly, both the Council and Police Commission inquisitions slammed to a halt at exactly the same time.

Perhaps it was just a coincidence but it certainly appeared the whole campaign to oust Lum was being orchestrated by the mayor.

There were growing indications Mayor Baptiste believed he could get rid of Lum before either the County Council or Police Commission investigations would start.

Baptiste had decided to use his pals on the Kauai County Ethics Board to remove his opponents on the Police Commission.

Baptiste would then appoint police commissioners who would do his bidding.

The year before, Carol Furtado's appointment to a second term on the Police Commission was held up for months by the County Council.

When she finally received a (closed, of course) confirmation hearing, according to numerous sources, she was rubber-hosed by many of the Council members led by Mel Rapozo, who is Furtado's cousin, and Council Member Sheylene Iseri-Carvalho, a former county prosecutor and close friend of Leon Gonsalves who had been an investigator for the County Prosecutor's Office.

Furtado, who repeatedly has shown she has a backbone of steel, never flinched.

Finally, she was confirmed.

On May 3, 2006, the Ethics Board conducted its hearing on the ethics charge against Furtado, alleging she had made the selection process that resulted in Lum being named chief unfair.

Unlike Ching, however, Furtado had opposed Lum's appointment as acting chief, which was the basis for the hearing officer's finding against Ching.

Furtado later supported Lum for appointment as the permanent chief.

Furtado, who appeared without an attorney, waived her right to a closed hearing and accused the mayor, the County Council, Gonsalves and even the Board of Ethics of conspiring in a "smear campaign" against Lum.

Furtado conceded Lum was "not the popular choice" among the Hawaiian and Japanese middle managers on the KPD who, in turn, are well connected with several Council members.

But she was sharply critical of Baptiste using the Ethics Board to get rid of Lum by kicking Lum's supporters off the Police Commission.

"They're hunting Lum by trying to get rid of me. It's not going to end here. It will continue. If I am cleared, they will find someone else," she told the Ethics Board.

"They are looking for someone to crucify to get the end result, which is the removal of K.C. Lum," she added.

Furtado remained on the Police Commission.

Meanwhile, the County Council in late May took up an Ethics Board finding that Deputy Chief Ron Venneman had violated ethics rules by helping circulate a petition to the Police Commission backing Lum as the best candidate for chief.

The petition was signed by 100 officers, about three-fourths of the department.

Venneman did not deny circulating the petition and said it was within his First Amendment rights to do so.

However, the Ethics Board's hearing officer, again John McConnell, held Venneman had breached ethics rules by entering areas closed to the public to obtain signatures from police officers.

As he had ruled with Ching, McConnell did not find Venneman broke any laws.

Hawaii does not have a Little Hatch Act, which exists in many states. Like the federal Hatch Act, Little Hatch Acts prohibit public employees from engaging in politics.

In Hawaii, public employees engaging in politics is perfectly legal. What Venneman did was legal. But, once again, the mayor's Ethics Board ruled he had violated the ethics rule prohibiting his use of a public position to benefit himself or others, a very broad interpretation.

The Council sent a recommendation to the Police Commission that Venneman be fined $1,000 and demoted. Venneman, as of this writing, is a lieutenant working in the Traffic Division.

Meanwhile, Baptiste—through his administrative assistant and chief hatchet man Gary Heu—had advised Lum that on June 8, 2006, Lum's contract with the county would be terminated.

Not because of anything Lum had done.

But because the Ethics Board found that Mike Ching had violated the ethics rules—not the law—in supporting Lum's appointment.

In the very convoluted reasoning of the Baptiste Administration, that allowed the mayor to terminate Lum's contract.

Never mind that under the County Charter the police chief could only be hired and fired by the Police Commission.

Never mind that all of the other Police Commission members (except Gonsalves, of course) voted for Lum and their support had not been found to violate the Ethics Code.

The point was, as Lum later said, that Bryan Baptiste and the County Council have endless funds to hire lawyers to defend the most absurd legal theories.

Individual citizens, including police chiefs, have only limited resources to carry on court fights even if they are in the right and the government is in the wrong.

Lum retired as of June 7, 2006.

. . .

CHAPTER 23: KPD TIME BOMBS

While Baptiste played king and Rapozo pretended he was Joe McCarthy, new lawsuits were stacking up against the Kauai Police Department alleging incompetent and unethical cop conduct.

Both Baptiste and Rapozo were posing as KPD "reformers" but the fact was that when the local officers on KPD were burned, neither made any speeches about the lack of discipline or professionalism on the department.

Their "reforms" were limited to getting K.C. Lum out of office.

(The author had retired and moved from Kauai before these events took place. The information on these cases came from published news reports.)

In January 2006, an elderly couple filed a lawsuit against two KPD officers and Kauai County for allegedly throwing them to the floor and pointing guns at their heads in a marijuana raid on March 15, 2005.

Problem was, officers Scott Kaui and Damien Mendiola had the wrong house.

They then raided a second house, which also turned out to be the wrong house. The occupants of that house filed a claim for damages with Kauai County.

At the third house, they finally got the right place and arrested three men.

William and Sharon McCulley of Omao claimed in their lawsuit that Kaui and Mendiola watched a man in a Toyota truck pick up a box believed to contain marijuana from the post office and drive to a private road that has access to seven different houses.

The KPD officers didn't actually see the box being delivered, so they guessed the box was delivered to the house where the McCulleys were babysitting their grandchildren.

They guessed wrong.

Sharon McCulley claimed the officers burst into the house and Mendiola threw her to the ground, handcuffed her and pressed his gun to her head.

William McCulley, who walks with the aid of a walker, was thrown to the floor by Kaui. That set off an implanted device that is supposed to alleviate his back pain by sending an electric shock to his spine. The device went off repeatedly sending McCulley into uncontrollable spasms.

The two KPD officers then tried the second of the seven houses on the road and guessed wrong again.

The third time was the charm. They found the box and arrested David Hibbit who later pleaded guilty to first-degree promotion of marijuana, according to press accounts.

In November 2006, the Kauai County attorney asked the County Council for yet another $200,000 to hire outside lawyers to defend the county and the KPD in two separate cases.

The Council took up the request in executive session because the lawsuit involved a county employee and the matter thus qualified as a personnel matter, under the county attorney's logic.

The lawsuit stems from one of two similar cases in which the KPD allegedly planted drugs and drug paraphernalia on innocent people.

Prosecutors dropped the criminal charges in both cases after acknowledging KPD Sgt. Danilo Abadilla planted crystal methamphetamines in a car and two separate homes.

According to *The Garden Island*, the local newspaper on Kauai, Abadilla had been demoted but was still working as a patrolman on Kauai in 2006. The drug planting incidents took place in 2004 and 2005.

The lawsuit was filed in federal court in June 2006 by Dominador Lopez, Anastacia Lopez, and the estates of Jovencio Lopez and Analyn Manzano.

The lawsuit claims KPD searched the home of Rizal Balgos in July 2003 and seized crystal methamphetamines and drug paraphernalia.

Balgos then agreed to become a confidential informant for the KPD and worked for Abadilla, a member of the vice squad.

According to the press account of the lawsuit, in April, 2004, Abadilla ordered Balgos to plant drugs in Michael Olivas' car and then executed a search warrant for Olivas' vehicle and home.

Olivas was charged with second-degree promotion of a dangerous drug and possession and use of drug paraphernalia.

The case was continued at the request of prosecutors until November 2004 when county prosecutors offered Olivas a plea bargain in which he would admit guilt to a reduced charge of third-degree promotion of a dangerous drug.

Olivas rejected the deal and requested a preliminary hearing but the court session never took place. Instead, prosecutors suddenly dropped all the charges against him.

The second instance of Abadilla allegedly planting drugs and then exercising a search warrant to seize them came in June 2004, according to the press account of the lawsuit.

Again, Abadilla allegedly used Balgos to plant drugs and paraphernalia in a vehicle and the home of Dominadar Lopez and then signaled KPD officers to execute the search warrant they already had obtained.

The lawsuit claims KPD officers went into the home with guns drawn and seized the drugs that allegedly were planted.

As in the Olivas case, Lopez was offered a plea bargain in which he would admit to third-degree promotion of a dangerous drug but Lopez, like Olivas, demanded a trial.

A week before the trial, the charges suddenly were dropped. According to the lawsuit, a prosecutor told the Lopez family the drugs had been planted by Balgos.

The lawsuit contends the KPD knew of this and other cases where officers had illegally planted drugs but failed to discipline the officers involved.

Balgos, meanwhile, disappeared. Sources said he was a major drug dealer himself and had fled to the Philippines.

Once again, the Lap Dancing Incident was connected. Abadilla was a defense witness for Randy Machado in his 1996 trial.

· · ·

Just when everyone thought K.C. Lum's retirement as chief of the Kauai Police Department would end the most absurd chapter in the sorry history of Kauai County government, it got worse.

As he retired from the KPD, Lum announced he was a candidate for the County Council.

Figuring out exactly what happened next (why it happened is too obvious) from a wide variety of accounts, this appears to be the story:

On May 30, 2006, the Honolulu law firm representing Kauai County faxed a letter to Lum's Honolulu attorney, Clayton Ikei, informing Ikei that the county had decided to cancel Lum's contract as chief of police.

The letter also said Lum could serve as a lieutenant on the KPD if he wanted to remain on the force.

It directed Lum to contact Gary Heu, Baptiste's administrative assistant, within a week to let him know Lum's decision about the lieutenant position.

The law firm also sent copies to their client, Kauai County, including the mayor and the County Council.

Ikei scanned the faxed letter and attached it in an email to his client, Lum.

Lum sent an email to Heu declining the offer and attached the letter from the county's attorney. Or at least the version he received from Ikei.

Heu emailed Lum saying the letter Lum had attached in his email to him was not identical to the one the mayor's office received from the county's private attorney.

Missing were the two paragraphs about the offer of a lieutenant's position.

Ikei, Lum's attorney, admitted the mistake was his. In scanning the faxed letter from the county's lawyer there was some overlap of the pages and the two paragraphs were covered up.

Lum immediately sent out corrected versions with the missing paragraphs restored. He sent the corrected version within two hours of sending the original version.

In the meantime, Lum announced he would be a candidate for the County Council.

The Council incumbents' reaction reflected its natural tendency to retaliate harshly against its critics: Rule #1 includes "Punish Your Enemies."

At the Kauai County Council's June 15, 2006 meeting, Chairman Kaipo Asing went into one of his PowerPoint rants (which replaced his old blackboard chalk talk diatribes) accusing "someone" of tampering with a government document and publishing it on the internet to mislead the public.

The letter had been posted on an activist's website—the version without the paragraphs that offered Lum a job if he would accept a demotion. It was widely read throughout Kauai. And it made the mayor and Council look bad.

What happened next probably was a result of the stupidity of the activist who posted the wrong version of the letter on the Internet as it was of the Council's venomous attitude toward Lum.

It provided Council members an opportunity to lash out at Lum, who had the audacity to oppose them in an election. And, at the same time, they could thump on an incredibly clumsy activist.

Asing completely ignored the fact that Lum had sent a correction to everyone as soon as he was aware of the mistake, and his attorney took the blame.

And he ignored the fact that the original letter from the county's attorney had been in their hands from the start. So everyone knew what the entire letter said.

Nonetheless, the Council went into its anguish routine.

An editorial in *The Garden Island* newspaper gives a colorful account of the June 15 Council meeting:

"At that meeting Kaipo Asing, Jay Furfaro, Jimmy Tokioka and Mel Rapozo lamented the conspiracy of false information being foisted on the community by the posting of the document minus the paragraph, stating there was an open lieutenant position that Lum could apply for. Asing and his merry band were quite distraught at the blemish boiling to the surface on their untarnished reputations. 'The council does everything right, and then people do something that is not right and we get blamed for it,' Asing said.

"Tokioka hung his head low and sorrowfully said it was a shame that people would believe what they were reading.

"The media and the community are to blame for the council's tarnished reputation, lamented Asing. He was utterly disgusted that uninformed residents were actually speaking their minds when the only true authority on everything is the council. It was at that same meeting Asing, upset at a member of the public for asking the question about whether there are any charges against Lum, replied, 'We're not here to answer questions, we're here to take testimony.'"

But then it got nasty, also Standard Operating Procedure for Kauai's County Council, which habitually retaliates with all the subtlety of a train wreck.

On Sept. 14, only a week before Kauai's primary election, agents of the Hawaii Attorney General's Criminal Division served a warrant on Lum, searched his house and two vehicles, and seized his computer and three hard drives.

Lum was informed he was being investigated on a charge of altering a government document. The charge supposedly had been filed by the Kauai County Council—in other words, the people Lum was running against in the election—and the affidavit providing probable cause for the issuance of the search warrant is believed to have been signed by Asing.

The search warrant specified the search was to be conducted on or before Sept. 23, which was Election Day.

Of course, "the media was alerted" by the incumbent Council members whom Lum was challenging.

And, of course, Lum lost the election.

On June 29, 2007, nine months after it was seized, the Attorney General's Office returned the computer to Lum. Along with it came a letter informing him there would be no prosecution on the altering records complaint and that the case was closed.

There was no apology. The Republican governor had taken care of her Republican mayor on Kauai.

· · ·

When Lum resigned, Lt. Clayton Arinaga became acting chief. Arinaga had been publicly critical of both Lum and Venneman. He was one of the leaders of the old guard.

Arinaga is a graduate of Kapaa High School, a diploma neither Lum nor George Freitas ever could nail on their office wall.

Arinaga chose Lt. Gordon Isoda, another old guard stalwart, as his acting deputy.

The department had been cast back into the Dark Ages where terms like "diversity" and "Constitutional rights" couldn't be found in the KPD vocabulary. And that's just where Baptiste and the County Council seem to want the KPD.

As usual, the whole show was scripted in advance and the outcome assured.

Arinaga said he didn't want the permanent appointment, so the County Council coughed up even more money to patch up the police department: $50,000 for a head-hunter firm to come up with candidates.

Nothing gets done in Kauai County government unless it goes to an expensive outside consultant or lawyer. And, since the consultant or lawyer never is from Kauai, there is a message there somewhere about the lack of competency in Kauai County.

In July, 2007, the recruiting company, after searching the entire planet (perhaps even the entire solar system), sent Kauai County its list of recommendations.

The three finalists included former HPD Major and Kauai native Darryl Perry.

Darryl Perry, a Kauai native and retired Honolulu Police Department major, was the choice of the Mayor Bryan Baptiste, the County Council and the middle management of KPD to replace Chief George Freitas, who was forced out by Baptiste. The Police Commission chose K.C. Lum instead. So, Mayor Bryan Baptiste used his Ethics Commission to get rid of the Police Commission chairman who supported Lum and then declared Lum's contract was invalid. Once the chief's office was vacant, Perry got the job.

The important thing to know about consultants hired by politicians is they have to agree to arrive at the conclusions the politicians want before they begin their study. Otherwise, they wouldn't be hired.

This is the same Darryl Perry who was a finalist when Lum was selected chief. The same Darryl Perry who is a close friend of Leon Gonsalves. The same Darryl Perry who was born on Kauai and was graduated from Kauai High

School. The same Darryl Perry who had briefly served on KPD but spent most of his police career in Honolulu.

A month later, Perry was appointed chief by a police commission stacked with Bryan Baptiste appointees.

The decade-long circle had closed. The KPD again had a local chief. And no one is interested in discussing racism and sexism in the department.

In fact, Mayor Baptiste again rewarded racist comments.

After the County Council refused to honor Bryan Baptiste's bogus request that they fire Gonsalves from the Kauai Police Commission, Gonsalves served out the remainder of his term.

Then Police Commissioner Gonsalves was re-appointed, by Baptiste, to a second term. Wasn't this the same guy Baptiste had asked the Council to remove during his initial term? No one on the Council asked.

And there was no mention of Hop Sing or Little Joe when the Council approved Gonsalves's second term.

. . .

CHAPTER 26: WHAT BODDAH YOU?

"What boddah you?" is a Hawaii Pidgin expression meaning, literally, "What is bothering you?" or "What is your problem?" or "What are you upset about?"

"It's the United States, but it's not America," a former newspaper editor on Kauai is fond of saying.

Another veteran Kauai journalist puts it this way:

"Kauai is like the Wild, Wild West. The Constitution and the laws only apply here when it's convenient. Otherwise, they make it up as they go along."

Kauai lies 100 miles to the northwest of and 100 years behind the rest of the 50th state. Kauai is the most remote and the least developed (in every way) of the main Hawaiian Islands.

Look up the word "insular" in the dictionary and there is Kauai: 1) Suggestive of the isolated life of an island. 2) Circumscribed and detached in outlook and experience; narrow or provincial (The American Heritage Dictionary of the English Language).

Tourists like to pretend they "discover" Kauai: Rural and quaint and, of course, stunningly beautiful. They take home pretty pictures.

Visiting Kauai is like dining at a fine restaurant. The ambience is superb. The food tastes delicious.

But, unless the yelling is especially loud that evening, tourists never would guess at the mayhem going on back in the kitchen.

Bigotry and racism, of course, exist throughout the United States and the world. What makes Kauai particularly unique is that racism, sexism and bigotry are ignored, indeed applauded, both officially and as a cultural norm.

Discrimination on Kauai is exactly the opposite of the racism found on the mainland. On Kauai, brown-skinned people are the majority and (for now, but not for much longer) whites are the minority.

Racism in any form is just as ugly.

Discrimination never is discussed on Kauai. It never is written about. No one wants to admit it exists.

In the recorded history of Kauai, no county employee ever has been disciplined for making racist comments or showing favoritism to locals with brown skin while discriminating against *haoles* with white skin.

To the contrary, discrimination and bigotry are rewarded in Kauai County government. Racism is what keeps Kauai's politicians in office.

Consider this:

The overall labor force on Kauai is 40 percent white but only 8 percent of the employees in Kauai County government are Caucasian.

A visitor can walk around the Kauai County Building all day without seeing a white face.

Much more important: It is equally true that 60 percent of Kauai voters are local (meaning native Hawaiians and descendants of sugar workers, almost all with brown skin), not white.

And local—not white—approval is what Kauai's politicians seek because, after all, the majority rules. So the government jobs all go to locals, and they and their families and friends and neighbors all remember that on Election Day.

What politics really is all about, always and everywhere, is power. The key to winning an election—and thus power—on Kauai is pandering to local voters and their dislike and distrust of outsiders.

That is the context in which the KPD exists. The police—a club that on Kauai is almost exclusively local and almost exclusively male—are both a creation and a reflection of both the government and the island's society.

The KPD is run by and for locals. A *haole* police chief attempting to diversify the department is almost certain to run afoul of the local majority, and thus be opposed by politicians.

The inevitable result is a racist police department with a stamp of approval from Kauai County.

Government sponsored and approved racial discrimination is particularly hideous when it exists in the police department.

The KPD is the only county agency with the power to use deadly force, the power to incarcerate, and, especially, the power to intimidate.

The police also have the power to "look the other way" when a friend or relative is breaking the law. And, on Kauai, they often do.

Kauai County government operates outside the normal checks and balances designed into American democracy. There is no friction and no separation of powers between the executive and legislative and judicial branches of government. Everything is agreed on in illegal secret meetings. And the court on Kauai approves.

Even the press, the Fourth Estate, doesn't question. It serves as a lap dog rather than a watch dog. If there is a helicopter crash or a shark bite or a bursting dam, Honolulu reporters and photographers descend on Kauai in great herds. No expenses are spared to cover tragedy and catastrophe.

But coverage of social issues is considered "boring." It doesn't sell newspapers (at least in the minds of publishers, none of whom ever have worked a day in a newsroom).

And that is where the Hawaii press abdicates its most important role in a democratic society.

Kauai is the extreme example of a part of Hawaii stuck in the plantation past. It deserves inquiry.

Racial and ethnic conflict between locals and *haoles* is the single most dominant theme of life on Kauai, which is the furthest away, both geographically and socially, from the mainland United States.

In Asian-Pacific Islander culture, which dominates Kauai, the blade of grass that sticks up is cut off; the nail that sticks out is pounded in. Public acknowledgement of good deeds is just as bad as accusing a person of an evil act.

Asians and Pacific Islanders are much more likely to embrace leaders who are despots (as long as they remain reasonably benign).

If the island's political leaders (and its courts) can choose which laws to obey and which laws to ignore, there really is no cultural conflict in the minds of Kauai locals. It's perfectly acceptable. It's what's expected of the royalty (or *alii*, as the ruling class is called in Hawaii): They are free to make their own rules, at least up to a point..

It's democracy that's the stranger on Kauai. It's the *haoles*, the outsiders and activists and protestors who deviate from the Kauai norm.

"The *haoles* never stay very long," former Kauai Mayor Maryanne Kusaka is fond of pointing out, as though it is a criticism of white people. She openly advises employers on Kauai not to hire *haoles* and choose locals instead.

In fact, she should be asking why so many *haoles*—especially those with school-age children—leave Kauai. Maybe the answer lies in the way Kauai's locals treat the *haoles*.

"Kill *Haole* Day" has been outlawed in the public schools, officially at least, but the brown kids beat up the white kids on a regular basis and the KPD officers assigned to the schools conveniently look the other way. So the white parents pack up their children and move to the mainland where the schools are both better and safer.

Maybe the Kauai government should set the example for tolerance and sensitivity and inclusion—but it doesn't.

Bad government, bad schools and no opportunities (beyond making hotel beds and cutting resort lawns) result in what is called throughout Hawaii "The Brain Drain": The best and the brightest of Kauai's children flee the island for better opportunities in Honolulu or the mainland as soon as they can.

Those left behind suffer from a massive inferiority complex. Kauai locals feel disempowered when they deal with the ever-increasing number of whites buying property and developing subdivisions and condos for even more whites. There is an anger born of past injustices (mostly real and mostly by whites).

Locals on Kauai are terrified of change and the very traditional island rapidly is morphing into something they don't want: Becoming another Maui, over-commercialized and controlled by outside interests.

But that's the way the *haole* developers and their local token hirelings are pointing them. The local officials gladly cozy up to the developers in hopes of payoffs, much like the Hawaiian royalty sold their kingdom to outsiders two centuries ago.

Local culture becomes dysfunctional is when it is layered on democracy. It's just not a good fit, largely because the democracy never operates with all of the checks and balances it's supposed to have.

Locals show great deference to authority and never openly challenge it. It is not in their cultural heritage and in a place as isolated as Kauai, their assimilation into the American mainstream has been painfully slow.

Kauai is one of very few places in the United States where the citizens—with good reason—fear their government: Retaliation is essential for the government to keep the peasants in line.

The vast majority of Kauai's locals want to go through life unnoticed. Certainly they would never speak up to defy authority.

It's called "humility" but, in reality, it's an attempt at hiding, as anonymously as possible, within the herd, the flock or the pack.

The island is remote and ignored, especially by the Honolulu news media and state and federal prosecutors, which should be paying more attention because Kauai is unique in all the wrong ways and thus worthy of at least some minimal attention.

The overall culture in Kauai County government and at the KPD is racist and sexist and corrupt. And the local politicians keep it that way.

And the local voters keep returning the same politicians to office.

. . .

REGARDING SOURCES

Everything you read in this book is true. It all really happened.

But the story isn't *everything* that happened. It can't be and never will be *the whole story* because Kauai County government constantly defies both the spirit and the law of Hawaii's open meetings and public records statutes.

This book is limited to a series of snapshots of the KPD and Kauai County government, afforded only when events align to open windows for a peek inside. In particular, they are drawn from lawsuits against the county and its police department.

To be sure, they represent the worst of the abuses. There are some very fine officers at the KPD and many good people who work for Kauai County.

Perhaps the most dysfunctional aspect of democracy throughout Hawaii is the failure of the news media, particularly in Honolulu.

The third-world attitudes and practices of Kauai County officials traditionally go unchallenged by the Hawaiian press, while in most of the United States the press functions as the watchdog on government. Therein lies the problem.

When a public official illegally closes a conference room door or locks up public records, newspapers in most of the country immediately dispatch their lawyers to the nearest courthouse to force open those meeting rooms and filing cabinets.

On Kauai and, more importantly, in Honolulu, where the state's two major daily newspapers are published, the press is a willing and complacent lapdog of government. Newspapers and the electronic media only rarely take the government to court. In Kauai's local culture, no one dares criticize the monarch.

So, the primary sources for this book rarely are Kauai County records or interviews with Kauai County officials or their staff members, whose jobs depend on blind loyalty. On-the-record interviews with the mayor or county council members are exceedingly rare. Mayor Bryan Baptiste, in his entire first year in office, allowed only two interviews to any members of the press.

Kauai's government officials believe they have a right to operate in secrecy. And unless the press takes them to court and bloodies their noses with open meeting and public records lawsuits, they will continue to do so.

The interviews for this book were requested. The records were sought. But most were refused.

Instead, I relied very heavily on other public records outside the control of Kauai County government: Court documents.

During the decade covered by the book, Kauai County and the Kauai Police Department (KPD) were sued again and again by both citizens and the police department's own officers and employees. In almost every case, the county settled in order to avoid a public trial and testimony about how corrupt county government is.

The pleadings in those lawsuits, the case files, are public record. Unlike its own file cabinets, Kauai County can do nothing to block a journalist's access to court documents.

Most lawsuits against Kauai County were filed in federal court—the U.S. District Court in Honolulu—rather than in state court on Kauai. The reason was simple enough: The local state judge was much too friendly to the county.

The federal courthouse was the best source of available and accurate official documentation. So, this book focuses primarily on those lawsuits.

If it appears Kauai County's position—and the debate among county officials on formulating those public policies—sometimes is not fully discussed in these pages, it is only because the county refused to cooperate. County officials fought every attempt at access.

I certainly wish it were otherwise, because it is in my professional nature to provide a complete and balanced story. However, Kauai County elected officials repeatedly refused to cooperate.

It also will be obvious that the events related in this book involve a much broader perspective than the KPD. There is much discussion of the administrations of the two mayors and the conduct of the county council because it is only in the context of their self-imposed secrecy and blatant disregard for the rule of law that this story can be told.

The simple fact is that the woes of the KPD are symptomatic of a much broader problem: the lack of accountability of Kauai County's elected officials and the cronies and political hacks they appoint to key government posts.

There are efforts afoot to replace Kauai's "strong mayor" system (which never was intended for small, rural governments) with a "council-manager" form of government in which a professional administrator runs the county and the mayor's powers are limited to chairing council meetings and cutting ribbons.

The current "strong mayor" system has been an abject failure. Kauai County government and its elected leaders have for too long been totally out of control, hiding their corruption and their blunders in closed-door "executive sessions" and in locked files in constant violation of the state's sunshine laws.

Accountability to the public—to the voters who put them in office—simply does not exist in Kauai County. That's the way the mayor and the council members want it.

Historian Robert A. Caro, in his splendid multi-volume biography of President Lyndon Johnson, disputes the popular notion that "power corrupts, and absolute power corrupts absolutely."

Instead, Caro points out: *Power reveals the true nature of those who attain it.*

. . .

ABOUT THE AUTHOR

Tony Sommer worked as a daily newspaper reporter on Kauai for eight years, most of that time as *The Honolulu Star-Bulletin*'s entire Kauai bureau.

He holds a bachelor's degree with a major in journalism and a minor in political science from Central Michigan University (1967) and a master's degree in journalism and political science from Ohio University (1968).

Before moving to Hawaii, he spent 25 years as a reporter for *The Phoenix Gazette*, the city's afternoon daily newspaper, specializing in state government and legal issues. He covered the administrations of six Arizona governors, the Arizona Legislature and the Arizona Supreme Court.

He also worked three years as *The Gazette*'s investigative reporter covering Charles Keating and the largest savings and loan swindle in American history.

He was the *Gazette*'s Phoenix City Hall reporter twice, covering the administrations of two different mayors in the nation's fifth largest city.

Tony also has extensive experience as a police officer and administrator, an unusual background for a journalist and one which allowed him a unique perspective on the Kauai Police Department.

Commissioned in 1967 in the U.S. Army Military Police Corps, he left active duty in 1972 as a captain.

Among his active duty assignments, he was the Military Police Station commander at Fort Carson, Colo., for more than a year and deputy provost marshal (police chief) of the 4th Infantry Division (Mechanized) for a year and a half.

He remained in the active Army Reserve as a Military Police officer for another 23 years, retiring in 1995 as a lieutenant colonel. Among his reserve assignments, he commanded a battalion-level Military Police unit and was an instructor at the U.S. Army Command & General Staff College.

Tony retired from daily news reporting in 2005 and returned to Phoenix where he now writes on whatever interests him.

INDEX